Development Centre Studies

Jobs for Rural Youth

THE ROLE OF LOCAL FOOD ECONOMIES

This work is published under the responsibility of the Secretary-General of the OECD. The opinions expressed and arguments employed herein do not necessarily reflect the official views of the member countries of the OECD or its Development Centre.

This document, as well as any data and map included herein, are without prejudice to the status of or sovereignty over any territory, to the delimitation of international frontiers and boundaries and to the name of any territory, city or area.

Please cite this publication as:
OECD (2021), *Jobs for Rural Youth: The Role of Local Food Economies*, Development Centre Studies, OECD Publishing, Paris, https://doi.org/10.1787/692c0ca1-en.

ISBN 978-92-64-91717-0 (print)
ISBN 978-92-64-79467-2 (pdf)
ISBN 978-92-64-72497-6 (HTML)
ISBN 978-92-64-81556-8 (epub)

Development Centre Studies
ISSN 1563-4302 (print)
ISSN 1990-0295 (online)

Revised version, April 2022
Details of revisions available at: https://www.oecd.org/about/publishing/Corrigendum_Jobs-for-Rural-Youth.pdf

Photo credits: Cover © Design by the OECD Development Centre.

Corrigenda to publications may be found on line at: www.oecd.org/about/publishing/corrigenda.htm.
© OECD 2021

The use of this work, whether digital or print, is governed by the Terms and Conditions to be found at https://www.oecd.org/termsandconditions.

Foreword

Rural youth today constitute the majority of the youth population in many developing countries. Most of them are engaged in subsistence farming and struggle to find better-paying jobs to escape poverty. It is becoming increasingly clear that rural youth are turning their backs on subsistence agriculture and aspire to better jobs elsewhere. Potential job opportunities for rural youth exist, however. Growing populations, urbanisation and rising incomes of the working class are increasing domestic demand for more diverse and value-added agricultural and food products in Africa and developing Asia. This rise in domestic food demand could boost job creation in the food economy if local food systems were mobilised to take up the challenge of higher and changing domestic demand for food. An important question, therefore, is how governments could make local food economies more vibrant so that they create a real market demand for local producers and all actors along the agri-food value chain.

This study places rural youth employment in developing countries at the centre of the analysis. It aims to sharpen our understanding of the challenges associated with current food systems in terms of decent job creation and environmental footprint and to explore which food production and distribution models are more likely to ensure not only economic gains but also social and environmental benefits. A key message is that integrating rural youth into productive and environmentally sustainable agri-food activities rooted in inclusive domestic food systems may well be one of the few lasting solutions to the current rural youth employment challenge. For this to happen, actions need to be taken today.

The findings contribute to the work of the OECD Development Centre on building more cohesive societies and helping countries to identify emerging issues and find innovative solutions to address social challenges. The research was undertaken with financial support from the European Union to provide evidence for the policy dialogue on youth well-being in developing and emerging countries. It is based on the analysis of data from selected developing countries in Africa and Asia, as well as a review of different local food models across the world.

This work adds to the policy dialogue on rural youth employment in three essential ways. First, it constitutes an important effort to understand the structure of youth employment in the different segments of the food economy as well as the employment growth potential in the food economy under current food models at horizon 2030. Second, it takes stock of a number of local food systems and short food supply chain models commonly found in developed countries that reconcile economic, social and environmental objectives. Finally, it discusses the replicability of such models in the context of developing countries and proposes some policy directions that will be needed to harness the potential of rural youth through vibrant, sustainable and inclusive domestic food systems anchored in local and regional value chains. We hope that this study will stimulate discussion among development stakeholders to bring about environmentally sustainable food systems that contribute to food security and work for the large number of rural youth in developing countries.

Acknowledgments

Jobs for Rural Youth: The Role of Local Food Economies was prepared by the OECD Development Centre under the overall guidance of Director Ragnheiður Elín Árnadóttir and Deputy Directors Federico Bonaglia and Ayumi Yuasa. Alexandre Kolev, Head of the Social Cohesion Unit and Ji-Yeun Rim, Senior Policy Analyst supervised and co-ordinated the project. The report was drafted by the Social Cohesion team: Alexandre Kolev, Ji-Yeun Rim, Justina La and Antoine Bonnet with research assistance from Sarah Karam, Antonela Leiva, Toma Savitki and Shirsha Sen. The report was edited by Jill Gaston and prepared for final publication by Aida Buendia, Delphine Grandrieux and Elizabeth Nash.

The report benefited from technical inputs from internal OECD colleagues, international organisations, United Nations agencies, research institutes and non-governmental organisations working on rural youth employment and agri-food value chains in developing countries. The contributions from the following individuals are gratefully acknowledged: OECD Development Centre colleagues Henri-Bernard Solignac-Lecomte, Senior Communications Manager; Arthur Minsat, Keiko Alvarez and Bakary Traoré of the Africa Desk; and Vicente Ruiz and Semhar Haile of the Territorial Development Unit; and Philipp Heinrigs of the Sahel and West Africa Club; Koen Deconinck of the OECD Trade and Agriculture Directorate; Anna Befus, Maria Lee and Marwan Benali of the Food and Agriculture Organization of the UN; Pierre Girard of ART-Dev Research Unit at CIRAD; Leonard Mizzi, Willem Olthof and Conrad Rein of the Rural Development, Food Security, Nutrition Unit at the European Commission.

The study's research concept and draft results were presented and discussed on 24 January 2020 at the OECD in Paris; on 12 February 2021 at the meeting of the European Union Heads of Agriculture, Rural Development and Food and Nutrition Security departments to share preliminary findings; and on 17 June 2021 at an expert meeting on the findings of the report. The participation and contributions of the following experts are gratefully acknowledged: David Asare Asiamah, Founder of Agro Mindset Ltd., Ghana; Lebogang Botsheleng of the Department of Agriculture Land Reform and Rural Development of South Africa; Laurent Cortese of the Education, Vocational Training and Employment Sector of Agence française de développement; Nadine Gbossa of the International Fund for Agricultural Development; Josphat Gathiru Muhunyu of the State Department for Crop Development and Agricultural Research, Ministry of Agriculture, Livestock, Fisheries and Cooperatives of Kenya; and Fati N'zi-Hassan of the Africa Union Development Agency.

This report is co-financed by the European Union.

Table of contents

Foreword 3

Acknowledgments 4

Executive summary 8

1. Where tomorrow's jobs are: Feeding local and regional markets 11
    References 14

2. The food economy today: Low productivity and bad jobs 17
    Employment in the food economy 18
    Youth employment in the food economy 20
    Working conditions: Informal and vulnerable employment, earnings, and skills mismatch 23
    Rural versus urban food economy 28
    Young women in the food economy 29
    COVID-19, youth and the food economy: Focus on South Africa 34
    Conclusion 36
    Notes 36
    References 37

3. Booming demand: A new dawn for local food economies 39
    The emergence of a "global middle class" and rapid urbanisation 40
    Employment forecast in the food economy 43
    Evolution of the downstream sectors of the food economy 46
    Conclusion 50
    References 51

4. Turning local food economies into engines for more and better jobs 53
    Livelihoods and environmental challenges of current food systems 54
    The challenge with upgrading from low value-added to high value-added participation in agri-food global value chains 56
    The domestic and regional food market opportunity 59
    The contribution of different local food system models in advanced economies 61
    Conclusion 73
    Notes 74
    References 74

5. Policy options to stimulate local food economies — 83
Overcoming economic barriers — 84
Overcoming social barriers — 86
Overcoming environmental barriers — 86
Notes — 89
References — 89

Annex A. Methodological annex — 91
A. Methodology for the descriptive statistics on youth employment in the food economy (Chapter 2) — 91
B. Methodology for the employment forecasting (Chapter 3) — 95
References — 97

Tables

Table 2.1. Median hourly wage for food economy and non-food economy youth in local currency unit, in selected African and Asian countries — 28
Table 2.2. Median hourly wage of food economy youth by gender and food economy segment, in local currency units, in selected African and Asian countries — 30
Table 4.1. Evolution of female and youth employees within co-operatives in selected developing countries — 63
Table 5.1. Overview of policy implications for local food economies — 88

Table A A.1. Descriptive information on countries in the study — 91
Table A A.2. List of sample countries — 94

Figures

Figure 2.1. Percentage of food economy employment in total employment in selected African and Asian countries — 19
Figure 2.2. Distribution of total food economy employment by economic sector in selected African and Asian countries — 19
Figure 2.3. Distribution of workers in all food economy jobs in selected African and Asian countries, by age group — 20
Figure 2.4. Percentage of youth-held food economy employment in total youth employment and distribution between primary and secondary jobs, in selected African and Asian countries — 21
Figure 2.5. Distribution of youth-held and non-youth-held food economy jobs by broad segment, in selected African and Asian countries — 22
Figure 2.6. Distribution of youth employment across food economy segment, by level of education, in selected African and Asian countries — 23
Figure 2.7. Prevalence of informal employment amongst youth food economy jobs, in selected African and Asian countries — 24
Figure 2.8. Percentage of youth informal food economy jobs by status in employment, in selected African and Asian countries — 25
Figure 2.9. Distribution of food economy employment by economic sector, in selected African and Asian countries — 26
Figure 2.10. Percentage of mismatched youth in the food economy by food economy segment, in selected African and Asian countries — 27
Figure 2.11. Distribution of youth employment across food economy segments by location of residence, in selected African and Asian countries — 29
Figure 2.12. Distribution of young men and young women by food economy segment, in selected African and Asian countries — 30
Figure 2.13. Distribution of food economy jobs held by adult women and young women, by food economy segment, in selected African and Asian countries — 31
Figure 2.14. Distribution of young women in the food and non-food economies by educational attainment, in selected African and Asian countries — 32

Figure 2.15. Distribution of young women across food economy employment by level of education, in selected African and Asian countries — 33
Figure 2.16. Difference in total employment and total food economy employment between quarters 1 through 3 of 2019 to 2020, in South Africa — 34
Figure 2.17. Difference in youth food economy employment by informal status between quarters of 2019 to 2020, in South Africa — 35
Figure 2.18. Difference in youth food economy employment by food economy segment between quarters of 2019 to 2020, in South Africa — 35
Figure 3.1. Projected number of individuals belonging to the global middle class at horizon 2030, by region, relative to the 2020 level — 41
Figure 3.2. Projected share of the population belonging to the global middle class at horizon 2030, by region — 41
Figure 3.3. Spending on food-away-from-home in Thailand and Viet Nam, by income class and urban/rural status — 42
Figure 3.4. Employment in the food economy, number of jobs, 2019 and 2030 — 44
Figure 3.5. Employment in the food economy, share of total employment, 2019 and 2030 — 44
Figure 3.6. Employment by food economy sector, projected change 2019-30, percentage change over initial level — 45
Figure 3.7. Employment in agriculture, share of total employment, 2019 and 2030, by country — 46
Figure 3.8. Employment in downstream sectors of the food economy, share of total employment, 2019 and 2030 — 47
Figure 3.9. Employment in food processing, shares of total employment, 2019 and 2030 — 48
Figure 3.10. Employment in food marketing, shares of total employment, 2019 and 2030 — 49
Figure 3.11. Employment in food-away-from-home, shares of total employment, 2019 and 2030 — 49
Figure 3.12. Contribution of each downstream sector to overall downstream employment creation, 2019-30 — 50
Figure 4.1. Agriculture labour productivity, by region, 2000 and 2016 (in constant 2004-05 USD) — 55
Figure 4.2. Agri-food global value chain participation index, by region, 1995, 2005 and 2013 — 57
Figure 4.3. Employment intensity of agri-food sectors in low income countries and in Côte d'Ivoire — 58
Figure 4.4. Local agri-food business models — 63
Figure 4.5. Evolution of Bioocoop revenues and employment — 68

Boxes

Box 4.1. Inclusive food retail distribution model: Biocoop, France — 67
Box 4.2. Linking local producers with consumers through the digital platform: Loco-Motivés in France — 70
Box 4.3. Sourcing local to support food aid programmes in Brazil — 71

Executive summary

Today, the highest proportion of the world's youth lives in Africa and Asia, with the majority in rural areas. In Africa, 10 to 12 million enter the workforce every year, but only about 3 million find jobs. Rural youth are particularly at risk of being caught in poor quality employment. Yet more and better jobs can be created for them: growing populations, urbanisation and rising incomes of the middle class are increasing demand for more diverse, value-added agricultural and food products. With adequate investments to build efficient local food systems, this rising demand can boost job creation along the local agri-food value chains.

Realising the potential of food economies in Africa and developing Asia requires meeting three main challenges. First, low pay and poor working conditions make it difficult for farmers to sustain their livelihoods and attract new entrants to agriculture. Second, the current trajectory of growth in agriculture is environmentally unsustainable, with intensive and extensive production practices leading to deforestation, soil erosion and resource depletion. Third, while participation in agri-food global value chains (GVCs) by developing countries is increasing, gains in terms of domestic value added and employment creation have been limited.

This study explores the extent to which local food economies could respond to the employment needs of youth in developing countries. First, it assesses employment structures within food economies, using household-level data for seven countries at different stages of development: Namibia, South Africa, Tanzania, Uganda and Zambia in Africa; Thailand and Viet Nam in Asia. Secondly, it provides an employment forecast for 2030 in the food economy for selected African and Asian countries. Finally, it reviews various local food systems and short food supply chain models in advanced economies to assess their pros and cons, and how they reconcile economic, social and environmental objectives.

In the countries studied, the food economy makes up an important share of total employment, especially in low- and lower-middle-income countries, where it ranges from around 50% to 90%. Young people (aged 15-29) make up to 45% of the labour force there on average, and mostly work in the agricultural production segment. In middle-income countries, however, the food service segment represents a large share of youth employment in the food economy. In terms of gender distribution, young men are more likely to be engaged in agriculture, while young women are more likely to work in downstream segments, i.e. trade and services.

The majority of food economy jobs are in rural areas, particularly in low-income countries. However, the share decreases as countries reach higher levels of development. In Namibia and South Africa, most of those jobs are actually held by urban youth. In all countries studied except Uganda, urban youth in the food economy have jobs in the downstream segments, although a non-negligible share of them also work in agriculture.

Jobs in the food economy are often informal and vulnerable. Youth working in this sector are more exposed to informal employment than adults, but also compared to youth in other sectors. Agricultural production is the most informal segment. The share of vulnerable jobs is also higher, with the majority of youth employed as contributing family workers or own-account workers. Earnings for youth in the food economy are lower than for youth in other sectors, with the lowest earnings in the agricultural production segment. The level of skills mismatch, both over- and under-qualification, is also high, which pushes down youth job satisfaction. Youth working in downstream segments tend to have higher levels of education and earn a higher income than those in agriculture, signalling the potential for the processing and service segments of the food economy to create higher-skilled and better-paying jobs.

The food economy job forecast for 2030 for 11 African countries (adding Côte d'Ivoire, Ghana, Mali, Niger, Nigeria and Senegal to the five initial ones) and the two Asian countries shows an increase in the total number of jobs. In sub-Saharan Africa, 115 million jobs could be created in the food economy by 2030, a 20% increase from 2019. That represents 12 million additional jobs in agriculture and 8 million in the downstream segments. The segments experiencing the highest increase are food processing by 21%, food marketing by 39% and food-away-from-home by 43%. In the two Asian countries, overall food economy jobs are expected to increase only slightly. The premise for the forecast was that income growth and rapid urbanisation will hasten the transition towards a higher consumption of meat, fruits and vegetables, compared to cereals, requiring a large shift in outputs. The estimation takes into account the GDP growth forecast, urbanisation rate and employment elasticities for each of the food economy segments.

In search of responses to the challenges of current agricultural production practices, and the difficulties in upgrading participation in agri-food GVCs, the study reviews local food systems and short food supply chain models in advanced economies: agricultural co-operatives, community-supported agriculture, food co-operatives (or "food co-ops"), e-distribution platforms, public procurement, and territorial branding and certification schemes. More specifically, it looks at their outcomes in terms of livelihoods for smallholder farmers, the quality of jobs and environmental impacts. Although all models promote local development, as well as fair remuneration to farmers, short supply chains, job creation, social cohesion, and organic or other environmentally friendly production practices, some succeed better than others. Food co-ops with a multi-stakeholder membership seem to work the best in terms of scalability, environmental impacts and job creation.

Adapting such models to build more efficient local food systems and create jobs for youth in developing countries, however, requires new, strategic, economic, social and environmental choices, including significant investment in agri-food supply chain infrastructure, regulatory reforms, and new skills strategies.

- Improving the livelihoods of farmers and smallholder producers requires technology transfers to support the adoption of new production methods; investing in infrastructure to improve rural-urban linkages, as well as access to physical and virtual markets; and creating efficient phytosanitary and hygiene regulations applicable to smallholder producers and local small and medium-sized enterprises (SMEs) in agri-food processing and services.
- Job creation in the food economy requires narrowing skills gaps and mismatch through vocational training, but also a stronger emphasis on agricultural research and development in regular school curricula.
- Supporting the growth of local SMEs will be critical for creating wage jobs. Regular dialogue with them, and the private sector more generally, will provide important information about labour market needs and allow for adapting training and curricula.
- Finally, environmentally friendly food production and distribution models need to be promoted via organic or agroecological farming practices and technological innovations, as well as by raising awareness of sustainable consumption and values associated with local and regional products.

1. Where tomorrow's jobs are: Feeding local and regional markets

Growing populations, urbanisation and rising incomes of the working class are increasing demand for more diverse and higher value added agricultural and food products in Africa and developing Asia. This rise in food demand could boost job creation for youth in the food economy if local food systems were mobilised to take up the challenge of higher and changing domestic and regional demand for food.

Today, the global youth population is at its highest ever and still growing. The highest proportion of youth lives in Africa and Asia, and a majority of them are in rural areas. The youth population is expected to increase in Africa, at least until 2050, when it could exceed 400 million. By 2030, some 375 million youth in sub-Saharan Africa are expected to be in the labour force (Losch, 2016[1]). Asia, with over 650 million, will remain the region with the highest proportion of youth population in 2050 (UN DESA, 2019[2]). With such a large number of new labour market entrants, the challenge is not only to create jobs but also good jobs.

Young people in rural areas face the double challenge of age-specific vulnerabilities and underdevelopment of rural areas. Such challenges include low or no access to quality education and vocational training, assets such as land and finance, and limited opportunities to participate in decision making. One in five rural youth in developing countries never attended school, making it even more difficult for rural youth to find work outside of low-skilled agriculture jobs (OECD, 2018[3]). The challenges are even greater for youth under 18, as there is often a gap in national legislation between the age for compulsory school and the legal working age. According to the *Global estimates 2020* by the International Labour Organization and the United Nations Children' Fund, 35 million youth aged 15 to 17 are in child labour (ILO and FAO, 2021[4]), and this age group falls largely through the cracks of youth employment programmes. This is of particular importance because investing in youth early has proven to be more cost-effective and to increase their chances of gaining access to decent employment in the future (ILO, 2015[5]).

While agriculture absorbs the majority of rural workers in developing countries, low pay and poor working conditions make it difficult to sustain rural livelihoods. The majority of agricultural workers work informally, in poor and dangerous conditions, with long hours, earning low and unstable incomes, and many of them have to combine more than one activity to make a living (Niu, 2013[6]). As a result, rural youth in developing countries do not want to farm like their parents, and seek jobs outside of agriculture (OECD, 2018[3]).

Potential job opportunities for rural youth exist in agriculture and along the agro-food value chain, however. Growing populations, urbanisation and rising incomes of the working class are increasing demand for more diverse and higher value added agricultural and food products in Africa and developing Asia. The demand for higher value added foods as well as other goods and services will create demand for off-farm labour, especially in agribusinesses, which tend to be better paid and located in rural areas and secondary towns (Christiaensen, 2020[7]). This rise in food demand could boost job creation in the food economy if local food systems were mobilised to take up the challenge of higher and changing domestic demand for food.

Agriculture plays a key role in African economies, and the sector has the potential to contribute significantly to production and employment in other sectors through processing and agriculture-related manufacturing and services. The import share of total food consumption in in sub-Saharan Africa was about 10% in 2017 demonstrating the centrality of domestic food supply chains in the region (Liverpool-Tasie, Reardon and Belton, 2021[8]). Nevertheless food import bills are on a rising trend, estimated at USD 37 billion in 2016 (FAO, 2017[9]) and USD 44 billion in 2021 (FAO, 2021[10]), while at the same time, total packaged food sales are growing annually at 13%, 28%, and 7% in low-income, lower middle-income and upper middle-income countries, respectively, compared to 2-3% in developed countries (Reardon and Timmer, 2012[11]). This is an opportunity to develop the domestic and regional agri-food industry that could create decent jobs in the sector, particularly for rural youth. Agricultural transformation through increased productivity and quality of African farms and support to agro-processing and other agriculture-related manufacturing and services could change this (ACET, 2017[12]). The midstream segments (processing, logistics and wholesale) can make up 30% to 40% of the value added in food value chains in developing countries (Reardon, 2015[13]).

In Southeast Asia, rapid urbanisation, dietary changes and export opportunities have transformed agriculture over the past decades. Over the past few decades, the region has sustained high growth rates and successfully reduced income poverty. One consequence of this rapid growth, however, is that the region reached worrying levels of environmental degradation while inequality is on the rise, both within rural and urban areas and between them (IFAD, 2019[14]). Despite the share of agriculture in GDP decreasing, many countries in the region are still majority-rural and agriculture continues to play a key role in poverty reduction and rural job creation. Therefore, how the sector links to the rest of the economy, through agri-businesses and the development of agri-food industry in the downstream, will determine its social (jobs and livelihoods) and environmental impact (IFAD, 2019[15]). Improving the competitiveness of agriculture will be crucial to ensure that the growth and transformation of the agri-food economy remains pro poor (IFAD, 2019[15]).

Strategies to develop the agri-food sector have often focused mainly on developing exports of cash crops, neglecting the large potential of the domestic market. Global value chains (GVCs), when coherent with sustainable development objectives, can facilitate the dissemination of sustainable technologies and practices and promote productivity and income growth across countries (FAO, 2020[16]). Agriculture trade is also increasingly organised within GVCs and participation in agri-food GVCs can have spillovers in terms of productivity improvements, production growth and livelihood improvement (OECD, 2020[17]). However, for many developing countries, particularly in Africa, participation in agri-food trade has been a lot about primary inputs in the low-value added stages of the GVC, resulting in their share of global trade in value added remaining small, with limited spillover to the domestic economy (AfDb, OECD and UNDP, 2014[18]; UNCTAD, 2018[19]). A global study estimating the gains from linking in GVCs in terms of net value-added exports shows that 67% of total global value created under GVCs accrue to OECD countries, 25% to newly industrialising countries and Brazil, Russia, India, China and South Africa and only 8% to all other developing countries and least developed countries combined (Banga, 2013[20]).

As an attempt to benefit more from their participation in global trade, many developing countries are looking at ways to upgrade in GVCs. Indeed, upgrading is necessary to increase the share of value added captured domestically (Kaplinsky, 2013[21]). However, upgrading participation in agri-food GVCs through higher value activities has proven to be difficult for new entrants from developing countries. Part of the difficulty lies in the limited productive capacities and infrastructure of these countries, while GVCs are dominated by a few players from advanced economies, who design value capture on their own terms (UNCTAD, 2018[19]). Successful cases of upgrading in horticulture trade can be found in Senegal and Kenya who entered the "high end" horticulture trade through contract farming and large estate farming by exporting firms (Maertens, 2009[22]; Muriithi and Matz, 2015[23]). However, spillover effects in terms of job creation have been rather limited, and employment in the horticulture sector is mostly nonwage, in the form of family labour (Munga et al., 2021[24]). In general, structural and rural transformation is slow in most African countries as they are not diversifying the commodity mix much (IFAD, 2016[25]).

Upgrading in GVCs via value added manufacturing does not necessarily create more jobs. There are large differences as to the level of direct employment creation and value added within agri-food processing industries. Sector-specific market characteristics and the type of technology used can be more or less capital- and skill-intensive. A specificity of GVCs in Africa is that the indirect employment effects tend to be small, as their spillovers on the local economy are usually limited (AfDb, OECD and UNDP, 2014[18]).

Another major challenge is that the current trajectory of growth in agricultural production is environmentally unsustainable in developed and developing countries alike. According to the Food and Agriculture Organization (FAO), one-third of farmland is degraded, up to 75% of crop genetic diversity has been lost and 22% of animal breeds are at risk. Seventy-five percent of the world's food is generated from only 12 plants and 5 animal species, making the global food system highly vulnerable to shocks

(Altieri and Koohafkan, 2008[26]). Globally, deforestation continues at an alarming rate, with some 13 million hectares of forests a year converted into other land uses between 2000 and 2010 (FAO, 2010[27]). Close to 90% of global marine fish stocks were fully fished or overfished in 2013 (FAO, 2016[28]).

Notwithstanding the positive effects on productivity growth of GVCs in the manufacturing sector, exporting through GVCs cannot be a panacea for developing countries (Pahl and Timmer, 2020[29]). The complexity associated with the possibility to move to higher-valued added segments of GVCs, and the sustainability challenge associated with current food production systems bring growing attention to alternative food system models that are inclusive of smallholders and environmentally-friendly. An important question, therefore, is to what extent local food systems will take up the challenge of higher and changing domestic demand for food, and which type of local agri-food systems shall be promoted.

Recognising the potential of local and regional food value chains in developing countries for domestic and regional markets, the present study explores the potential contribution of local food economies to decent employment creation and environmental preservation. Specifically, the study addresses the following three questions:

1. What is the current structure of employment for youth (15-29 years old) in the different segments of the food economy?
2. What is the potential of job creation and decent work in the different segments of the food economy, taking into account rapid urbanisation and changing consumption patterns?
3. Which local food production and distribution models seem most promising to ensure not only economic gains but also social and environmental benefits?

The rest of the report is organised as follows: Chapter 2 provides a detailed description of youth in the food economy for five African countries (Namibia, South Africa, Tanzania, Uganda and Zambia) plus two Southeast Asian countries (Thailand and Viet Nam). Chapter 3 provides an employment forecast in the food economy for sub-Saharan African countries, based on data from the five countries above and six additional ones as well as for the two Southeast Asian countries reviewed above. Chapter 4 reviews several local economic models commonly found in developed countries and discusses replicability and scaling-up issues in the context of developing countries. Finally, Chapter 5 looks at key economic, social and environmental bottlenecks and offers policy directions that could unleash local food economies.

References

ACET (2017), *African Transformation Report 2017: Agriculture Powering Africa's Economic Transformation*, The African Center for Economic Transformation, Accra. [12]

AfDb, OECD and UNDP (2014), *African Economic Outlook 2014: Global Value Chains and Africa's Industrialisation*, African Development Bank; Organisation for Economic Co-operation and Development; United Nations Development Programme, Paris. [18]

Altieri, M. and P. Koohafkan (2008), *Enduring Farms: Climate Change, Smallholders and Traditional Farming Communities*, Third World Network, Penang. [26]

Banga, R. (2013), *Measuring Value in Global Value Chains*, United Nations Conference on Trade and Development, Geneva. [20]

Christiaensen, L. (2020), *Agriculture, Jobs, and Value Chains in Africa*, World Bank, Washington, D.C. [7]

FAO (2021), *Food Outlook – Biannual Report on Global Food Markets*, FAO, Rome, http://dx.doi.org/10.4060/cb4479en. [10]

FAO (2020), *The State of Agricultural Commodity Markets 2020. Agricultural markets and sustainable development: Global value chains, smallholder farmers and digital innovations*, Food and Agriculture Organization of the UN, Rome, http://dx.doi.org/10.4060/cb0665en. [16]

FAO (2017), *Food Outlook - Biannual Report on Global Food Markets*, FAO, Rome. [9]

FAO (2016), *The State of World Fisheries and Aquaculture 2016. Contributing to food security and nutrition for all*, Food and Agriculture Organization, Rome. [28]

FAO (2010), *The Global Forest Resources Assessment 2010*, Food and Agriculture Organization, Rome. [27]

IFAD (2019), *An Outlook on Asia's Agricultural and Rural Transformation: Prospects and options for making it an inclusive and sustainable one*, International Fund for Agricultural Development (IFAD), Rome. [14]

IFAD (2019), *An Outlook on Asia's Agricultural and Rural Transformation: Prospects and options for making it an inclusive and sustainable one*, International Fund for Agricultural Development (IFAD), Rome. [15]

IFAD (2016), *Rural Development Report 2016: Fostering inclusive rural transformation*, International Fund for Agricultural Development, Rome. [25]

ILO (2015), *World Report on Child Labour 2015: Paving the way to decent work for young people*, International Labour Office, Geneva. [5]

ILO and FAO (2021), *Child Labour: Global estimates 2020, trends and the road forward*, International Labour Office and United Nations Children's Fund, New York, https://www.ilo.org/wcmsp5/groups/public/---ed_norm/---ipec/documents/publication/wcms_797515.pdf (accessed on 20 July 2021). [4]

Kaplinsky, R. (2013), "Global value chains in manufacturing industry: Where they came from, where they are going and why this is important", *Innovation, Knowledge, Development Working Paper*, No. 68, Open University. [21]

Liverpool-Tasie, L., T. Reardon and B. Belton (2021), ""Essential non-essentials": <scp>COVID-19</scp> policy missteps in <scp>N</scp>igeria rooted in persistent myths about <scp>A</scp>frican food supply chains", *Applied Economic Perspectives and Policy*, Vol. 43/1, http://dx.doi.org/10.1002/aepp.13139. [8]

Losch, B. (2016), "Structural transformation to boost youth labour demand in sub-Saharan Africa: The role of agriculture, rural areas and territorial development", *Employment working paper*, No. 204, International Labour Office, Geneva. [1]

Maertens, M. (2009), "Horticulture exports, agro-industrialization, and farm-nonfarm linkages with the smallholder farm sector: evidence from Senegal", *Agricultural Economics*, Vol. 40/2, http://dx.doi.org/10.1111/j.1574-0862.2009.00371.x. [22]

Munga, B. et al. (2021), "Industries without smokestacks in Africa: A Kenya case study", *Africa Growth Initiative at Brookings*, No. 31, Brookings Institution, Washington, D.C. [24]

Muriithi, B. and J. Matz (2015), "Welfare effects of vegetable commercialization: Evidence from smallholder producers in Kenya", *Food Policy*, Vol. 50, http://dx.doi.org/10.1016/j.foodpol.2014.11.001. [23]

Niu, S. (2013), "Promoting Rural Development through Occupational Safety and Health", *Rural Policy Briefs*, International Labour Organization, Geneva, http://www.ilo.org/asia/whatwedo/publications/ (accessed on 3 August 2018). [6]

OECD (2020), *Global value chains in agriculture and food: A synthesis of OECD analysis*, Organisation for Economic Co-operation and Development, Paris. [17]

OECD (2018), *The Future of Rural Youth in Developing Countries: Tapping the Potential of Local Value Chains*, OECD. [3]

Pahl, S. and M. Timmer (2020), "Do Global Value Chains Enhance Economic Upgrading? A Long View", *The Journal of Development Studies*, Vol. 56/9, http://dx.doi.org/10.1080/00220388.2019.1702159. [29]

Reardon, T. (2015), "The hidden middle: the quiet revolution in the midstream of agrifood value chains in developing countries", *Oxford Review of Economic Policy*, Vol. 31/1, http://dx.doi.org/10.1093/oxrep/grv011. [13]

Reardon, T. and C. Timmer (2012), "The Economics of the Food System Revolution", *Annual Review of Resource Economics*, Vol. 4/1, pp. 225-264, http://dx.doi.org/10.1146/annurev.resource.050708.144147. [11]

UN DESA (2019), *2019 Revision of World Population Prospects*, United Nations Department of Economic and Social Affairs, New York, https://population.un.org/wpp/ (accessed on 12 February 2021). [2]

UNCTAD (2018), *Trade and Development Report 2018: Power, Platforms and the Free Trade Delusion*, United Nations Conference on Trade and Development, Geneva. [19]

2. The food economy today: Low productivity and bad jobs

Using household and labour force surveys of seven developing and emerging economies in Africa and Asia, this chapter examines the size and composition of the food economy and the conditions under which youth are employed in the food economy. The chapter provides descriptive statistics about the quantity and quality of youth employment within the food economy for Namibia, South Africa, Tanzania, Thailand, Uganda, Viet Nam and Zambia. It includes a specific analysis on the impact of the restrictive policy measures taken in 2020 during the COVID-19 crisis on youth employed in the food economy, with a focus on South Africa.

Rising incomes and changing lifestyle and dietary choices are poised to transform agri-food systems across developing countries, with potentially large implications for the quantity and quality of youth employment. Rapid urbanisation is expected to shift employment off-farm and increase employment opportunities in manufacturing and services (Allen, Heinrigs and Heo, 2018[1]). In light of the demographic structure, particularly in Africa, youth will both drive these changes in consumption and make opportunities out of this evolving economic landscape. In 2020, youth (15-29 years old) in the five African countries of this study (Namibia, South Africa, Tanzania, Uganda and Zambia) represented on average 30% of the total population and 50% of the working-age population (UN DESA, 2019[2]). In the two Asian countries (Thailand and Viet Nam), youth represented around 25% of the total population, and 30% of the working-age population (UN DESA, 2019[2]). These are significant shares of the general and working-age population, which will place additional pressure on labour markets. Youth educational attainment and aspirations have risen over recent decades, increasing both skills and aspirations mismatch and decreasing levels of job satisfaction among youth.

For seven emerging and developing economies in Africa and Asia, this chapter examines the size and composition of jobs in the food economy and the conditions in which youth are employed in the agri-food sector. The chapter provides a broad description of youth in the food economy and their working conditions, with a focus on differences across rural and urban areas, and women in the sector. Finally, it includes a special focus on the impact of the lockdown measures taken during the COVID-19 crisis on youth working in the food economy in South Africa. Although some commonalities can be drawn from the seven countries, the countries differ widely in their level of human and economic development and thus feature different agriculture and food system characteristics. It is worth keeping in mind each country's socio-economic context when interpreting the results in this chapter (see Annex A for some basic socio-economic indicators by country).

Employment in the food economy

In the majority of the sample countries, food economy jobs account for at least half of total employment. Following the classification scheme outlined in Allen et al. (2016[3]) and in Allen, Heinrigs and Heo (2018[1]), the food economy encompasses food agriculture, food processing, food marketing and food-away-from-home (see Annex A for more information). We observe large disparities between upper middle- and low-income African countries, ranging from 12% in South Africa to 92% in Tanzania (Figure 2.1). In Thailand and Viet Nam, food economy employment accounts for about half of total employment (Figure 2.1).

Figure 2.1. Percentage of food economy employment in total employment in selected African and Asian countries

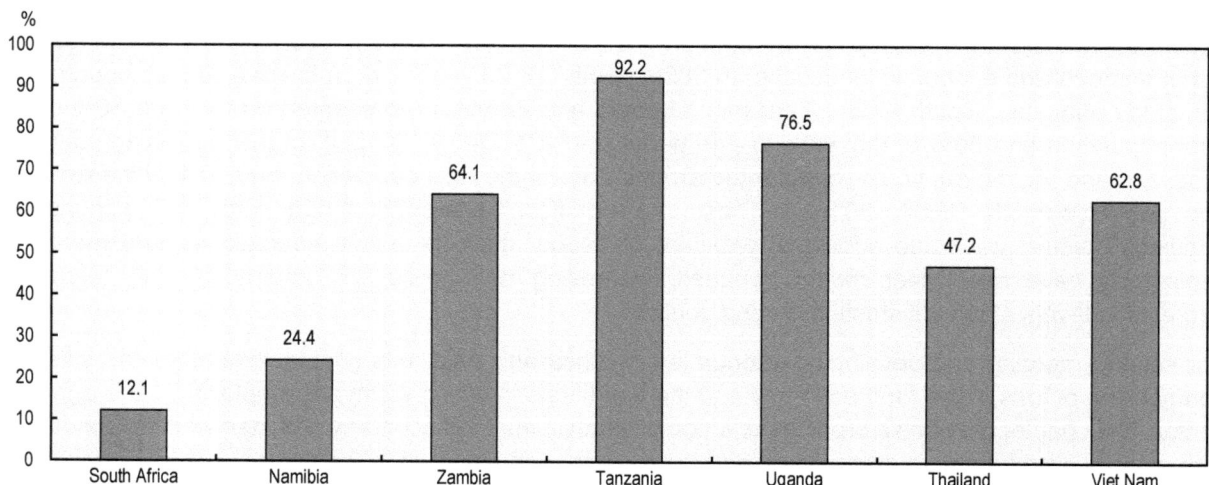

Note: Only primary employment is counted.
Source: Authors' calculations.

Agriculture makes up an important share, if not the vast majority, of food economy jobs. In the lesser developed African countries (Tanzania, Uganda and Zambia), food agriculture jobs encompass 88.1% to 92.3% of all food economy jobs. In Namibia, South Africa, Thailand and Viet Nam, the food economy is more diversified, with downstream activities taking up a larger part of food economy employment (Figure 2.2). The diversity of food economy activity appears to largely depend on the diversification of the broader economy.

Figure 2.2. Distribution of total food economy employment by economic sector in selected African and Asian countries

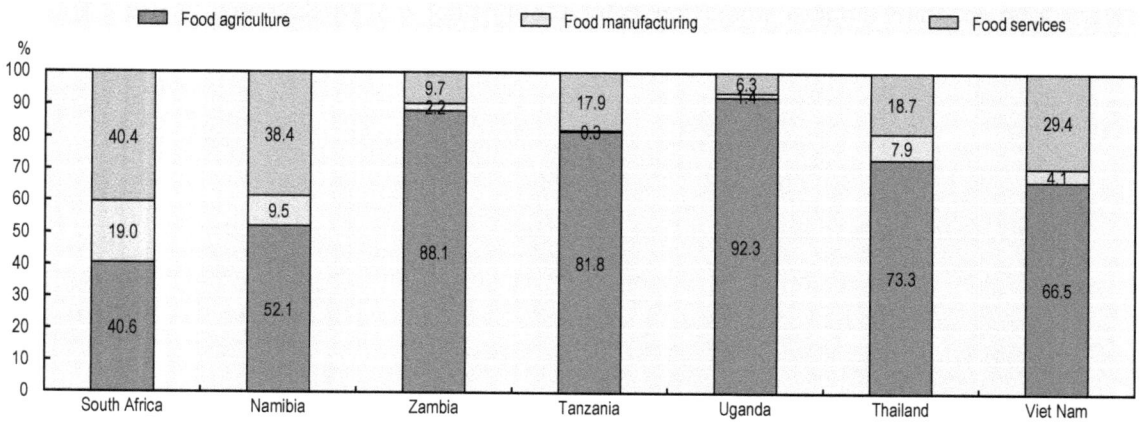

Note: Only primary employment is counted.
Source: Authors' calculations.

Youth employment in the food economy

Youth comprise a significant share of food economy workers, especially in the five African countries. Figure 2.3 shows the share of food economy workers in each age group. Except for South Africa, youth represent nearly 40% of food economy workers in the African countries studied. In the two Asian countries, the share of youth working in the food economy is relatively lower but remains significant (about 12.4% in Thailand and 20.5% in Viet Nam).

Figure 2.3. Distribution of workers in all food economy jobs in selected African and Asian countries, by age group

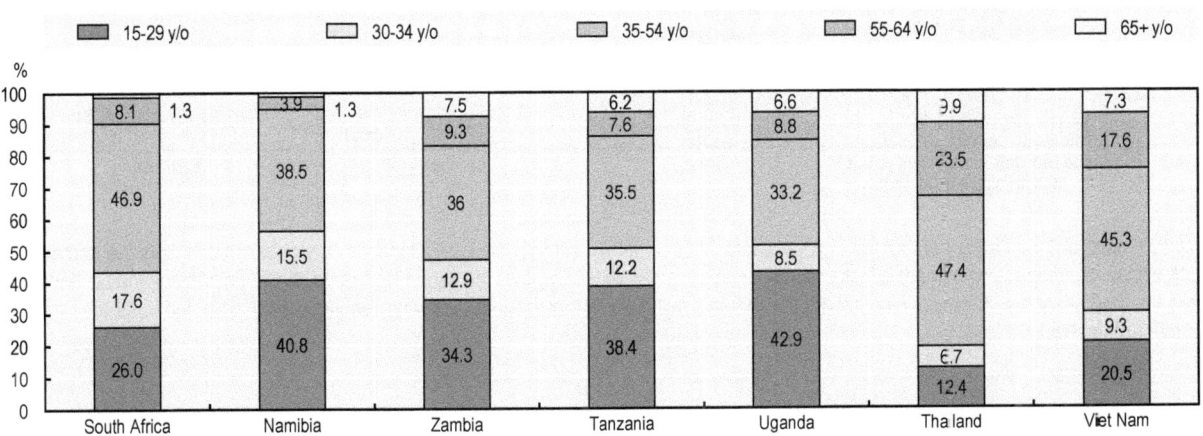

Source: Authors' calculations.

Working youth are likely to be employed in the food economy. In lower-income countries, 54% to 93% of youth are employed in food economy jobs (Figure 2.4). Youth have a lower rate of participation in the food economy in upper middle-income countries, ranging from 16% in South Africa to 37% in Thailand. In these countries, whose economies are more diversified, youth typically have higher levels of educational attainment, have greater aspirations and follow job opportunities in other sectors.

Food economy employment tends to be the primary employment of youth. For 90% to 97% of African youth, their jobs in the food economy were their primary employment. Youth in the two Asian countries hold jobs in the food economy as both their main and secondary employment, notably in Viet Nam (Figure 2.4).

Figure 2.4. Percentage of youth-held food economy employment in total youth employment and distribution between primary and secondary jobs, in selected African and Asian countries

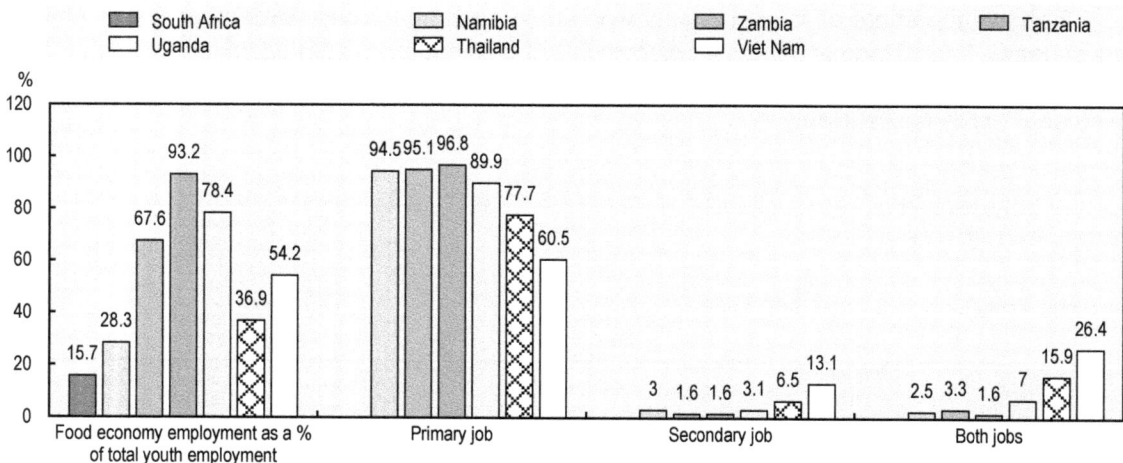

Note: "Primary job" shows the percentage of youth whose main employment is in the food economy; "Secondary job" shows the percentage of youth whose secondary employment is in the food economy; and "Both jobs" shows the percentage of youth whose primary and secondary jobs are in the food economy. Secondary job information was not available for South Africa. Primary, secondary and "both" job numbers total 100.
Source: Authors' calculations.

As is the case for adults, agricultural work remains the prevalent form of youth food economy employment. While this is especially true for lower-income countries, youth are finding more opportunities downstream in middle-income countries (Figure 2.5). In some middle-income countries (Namibia, South Africa, Thailand and Viet Nam), youth are more likely than adults to find jobs downstream, mainly in food processing and food-away-from-home. In a study examining youth participation in the agri-food systems of Africa, Asia and Latin America, Dolislager et al. (2021[4]) similarly find that youth are more likely than adults to work in a diverse range of food economy activities, outside of farming.

Figure 2.5. Distribution of youth-held and non-youth-held food economy jobs by broad segment, in selected African and Asian countries

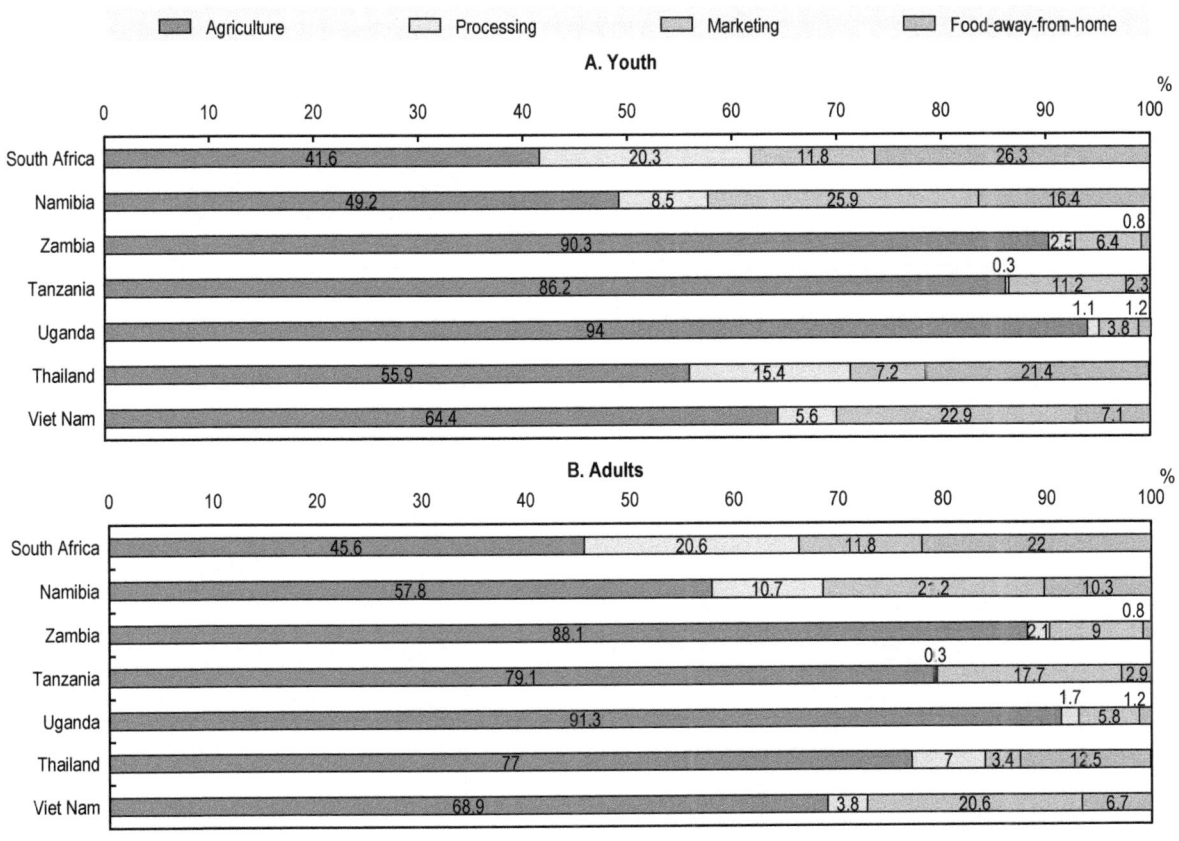

Source: Authors' calculations.

Agriculture remains a prominent employer for all levels of education, but educated youth have a higher probability of holding a job in downstream segments of the food economy (i.e. processing, marketing and food-away-from-home). Figure 2.6 shows the distribution of youth across their food economy segments, by their level of educational attainment. For each group, agriculture employs more than half of the youth who received either no schooling or only a primary or secondary education. Youth in Tanzania and Uganda are exceptions, where completing tertiary education was uncommon at the time of data collection. Thailand also presents an exception, wherein youth without a primary education also manage to find employment in downstream segments.

Figure 2.6. Distribution of youth employment across food economy segment, by level of education, in selected African and Asian countries

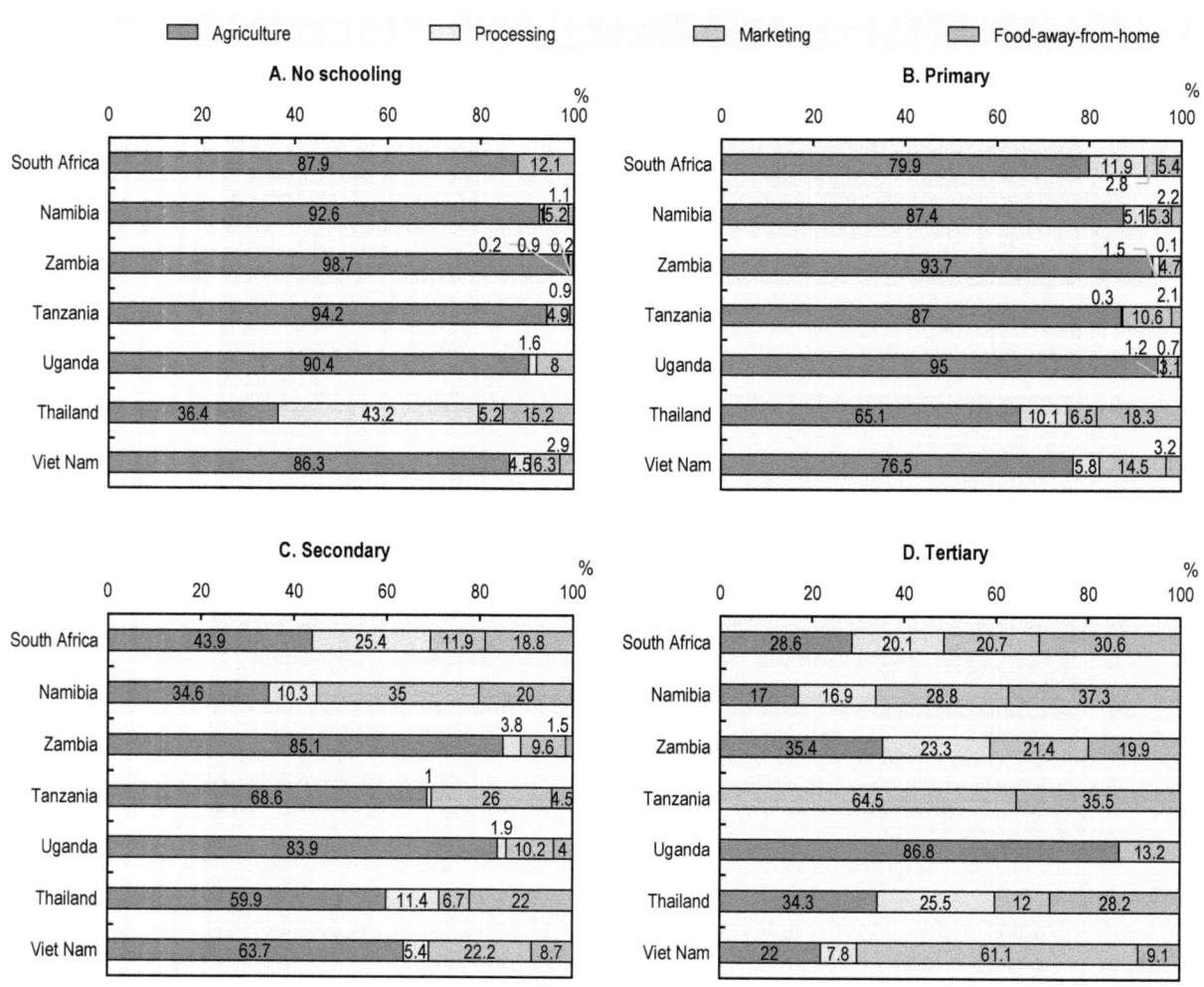

Source: Authors' calculations.

Working conditions: Informal and vulnerable employment, earnings, and skills mismatch

Many food economy jobs do not meet international standards on decent work, making Sustainable Development Goal (SDG) 8 difficult to reach. Decent work entails productive employment opportunities that pay fair income and protect workers, whether that protection is occupational safety and health standards in the workplace, through employment-based social safety nets, or the recognition and facilitation of collective bargaining rights. SDG 8 outlines a number of indicators and targets that should be measured to advance towards sustained, inclusive and sustainable economic growth that includes full and productive employment and decent work for all. SDG 8 encompasses cultivating decent jobs and entrepreneurship and formalising enterprises (Target 8.3); eradicating unfair pay discrimination (Target 8.5); eliminating child labour (Target 8.7); and protecting labour rights and promoting safe working environments (Target 8.8).

The majority of jobs in the food economy are informal. Informal jobs entail work that is undeclared and, therefore, unregulated and without social safety nets for workers. With the exceptions of South Africa and Thailand, the majority of youth-held jobs in each food economy segment are informal (Figure 2.7). The prevalence of informality among youth working in the food economy is higher than the informal employment rate in total employment. Informality is also highest in agriculture employment for all seven countries, but in the lower-income African countries, it is the norm in all segments of the food economy. This high incidence of informal work in the food economy warns that the majority of these youth are at high risk of vulnerability to poverty, of low job security, of no employment-based social insurance coverage and potentially of future vulnerability to poverty in old age, due to lack of employment-based retirement pension affiliation and contributions.

Figure 2.7. Prevalence of informal employment amongst youth food economy jobs, in selected African and Asian countries

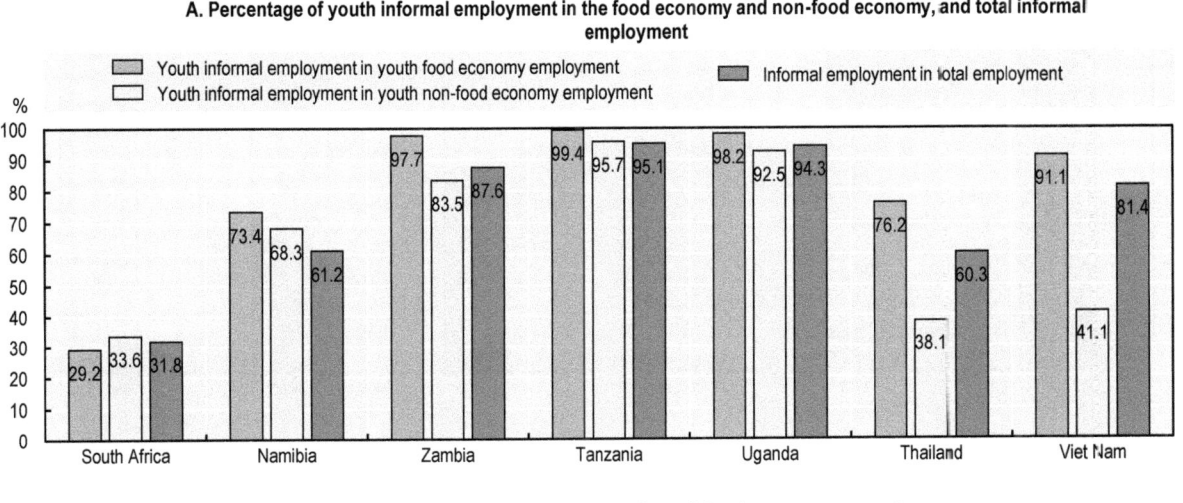

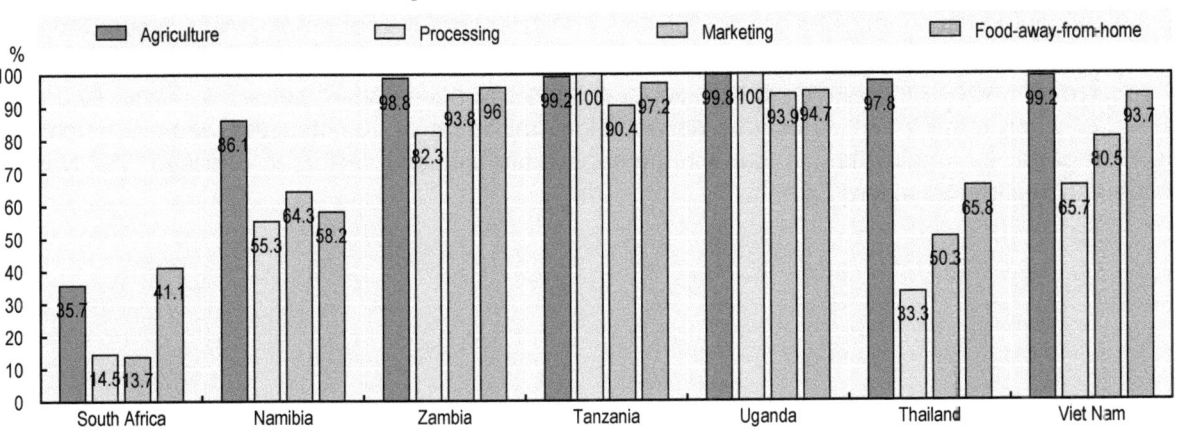

Source: Authors' calculations.

Most youth food economy workers hold vulnerable forms of employment. Own-account workers and contributing family workers are considered to have vulnerable employment, as they have less job and income stability than employees or employers, and contributing family workers are often unpaid. Almost no youth in the food economy is an employer, and the high prevalence of own-account and contributing family work confirms the poor quality of most food economy jobs and the difficulties youth face in securing gainful employment in this sector (Figure 2.8). These results are in line with a previous OECD study (2017[5]) that shows that very few youth in fact succeed as entrepreneurs or "agripreneurs" who are able to employ other people. Self-employed entrepreneurs are more likely own-account workers making a subsistence living. Successful youth entrepreneurs have very specific profiles, and therefore any youth entrepreneurship programme should target high potential youth so that their enterprises can create salaried jobs (OECD, 2017[5]). The majority of youth, especially rural youth, will not succeed as entrepreneurs, and it is important to manage expectations and not create unrealistic aspirations by overselling youth entrepreneurship as a panacea to the youth employment challenge (OECD, 2017[6]).

Figure 2.8. Percentage of youth informal food economy jobs by status in employment, in selected African and Asian countries

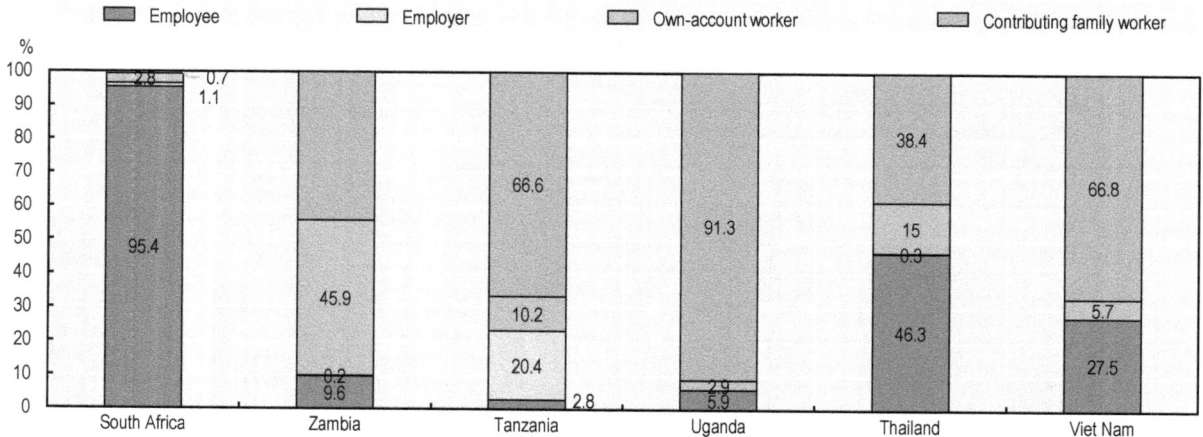

Note: Data not available for Namibia.
Source: Authors' calculations.

The majority of food economy jobs are not full-time equivalent or full-year employment. Figure 2.9 shows the differences within the set of all food economy jobs, wherein agriculture represents the lion's share of any employment when employment is defined as at least one hour worked per week (Panel A). Panel B shows that when employment is defined as working a minimum of 40 hours per week, a much larger proportion of gainful employment is found in the service and industry sectors in Thailand, Viet Nam and Uganda and to a certain extent Zambia.

Figure 2.9. Distribution of food economy employment by economic sector, in selected African and Asian countries

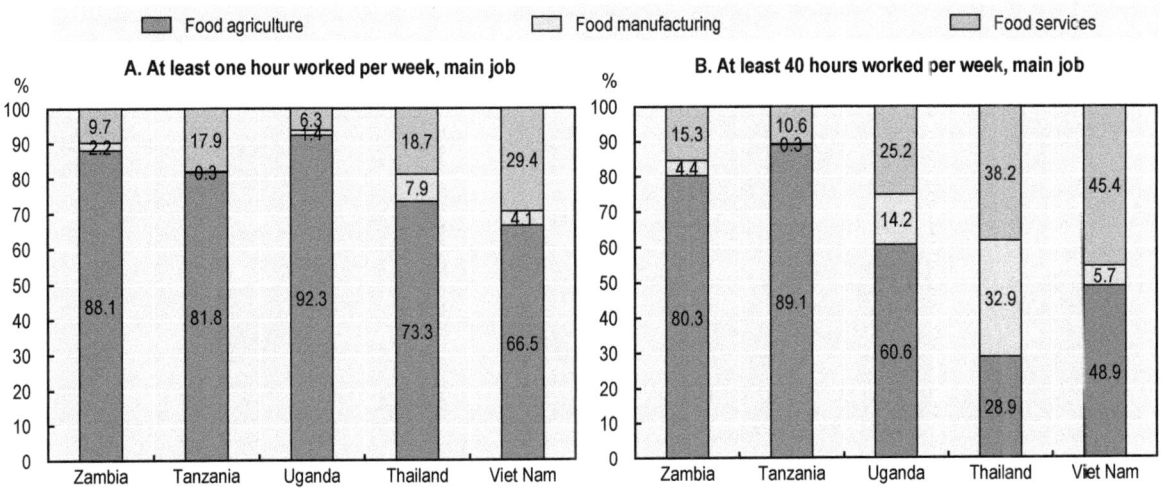

Source: Authors' calculations.

There is a high level of skills mismatch among youth in the food economy. Two-thirds of all food economy jobs held by youth do not correspond to their level of educational qualification. For the purposes of this study, youth are considered qualified according to the most frequently attained level of education in each occupational category, by country (ISCO-08). Just over one-third (40%) of all food economy youth are underqualified for their jobs, and just about one-quarter (24%) are overqualified (Figure 2.10).

Figure 2.10. Percentage of mismatched youth in the food economy by food economy segment, in selected African and Asian countries

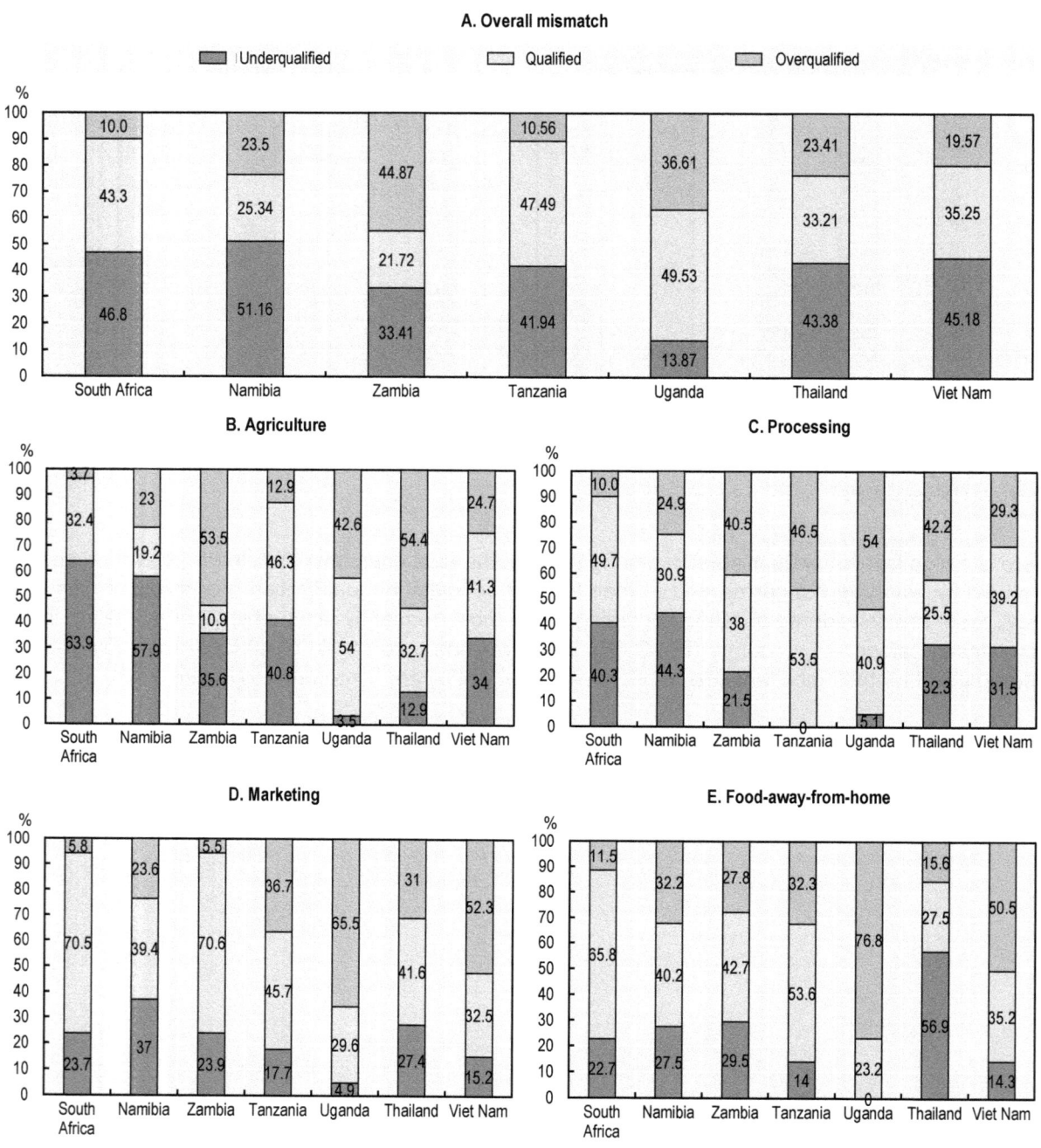

Source: Authors' calculations.

Youth working in the food economy earn less per hour than their counterparts working outside of the food economy. Table 2.1 displays the overall median hourly wage for youth working in and out of the food economy. Youth employed in the non-food economy earn more than both youth and non-youth working in the food economy. This is likely due to the influence of agricultural wages, which represent the majority of food economy jobs.

Food agriculture youth workers consistently earn the least, not only compared to youth outside the food economy, but also as compared to the earnings of youth in other food economy segments. In some cases, youth in downstream segments of the food economy can out-earn non-food economy youth, as observed in South Africa, Tanzania and Uganda (Table 2.1).

Table 2.1. Median hourly wage for food economy and non-food economy youth in local currency unit, in selected African and Asian countries

	South Africa	Namibia	Tanzania	Uganda	Thailand	Viet Nam
Food economy youth	18.3	5.8	684.3	787.3	39.4	17 307.7
Non-food economy youth	21.3	11.5	1 010.4	1 052.4	47.7	19 893.9
Agriculture	16.7	4.6	673.6	866.1	37.5	16 666.7
Processing	20.0	11.5	N/A	1 484.7	38.8	17 230.8
Marketing	22.9	6.8	1 837.9	787.3	48.1	19 098.1
Food-away-from-home	19.0	7.8	1 616.6	592.8	40.4	14 423.1

Note: Data not available for Zambia. N/A = not available.
Source: Authors' calculations.

Rural versus urban food economy

As with most economic activities, urban and rural food economies hold different employment prospects for youth. Rural food economy jobs are predominantly on-farm, whereas downstream activities thrive in urban areas. However, rural non-farm activity is also emerging in the middle-income countries in both regions, with around 20% (in Namibia, South Africa, Thailand and Viet Nam) of youth employment found in food processing, food marketing and food-away-from-home (Figure 2.11). Indeed, while traditionally there is a division between rural and urban food activities, there are often feedback loops between the two areas. Circular or seasonal mobilities often exist across these cities, with urban households having parts of their livelihoods in rural areas and vice versa (Allen and Heinrigs, 2016[7]).

Downstream food economy jobs held by youth are predominantly located in urban areas. Youth employment in the middle-income countries is characterised by low shares of jobs in agriculture, high shares of jobs in food-away-from-home, and variable shares of jobs in food processing and marketing. The more developed countries, South Africa and Thailand, have relatively high shares of urban food processing jobs; the lesser developed countries have much larger shares of urban food marketing (Figure 2.11).

Urban youth in the lower-income African countries (Tanzania, Uganda and Zambia) are predominantely involved in food agriculture or food marketing. Food-away-from-home represents less than 10% of urban food economy jobs in this group of countries who are also largely agrarian in transition. In Uganda, particularly, the share of employment in urban agriculture remains high (78%), which can be partly accounted for by low levels of urbanisation (22%) at the time of data collection (Figure 2.11).

Figure 2.11. Distribution of youth employment across food economy segments by location of residence, in selected African and Asian countries

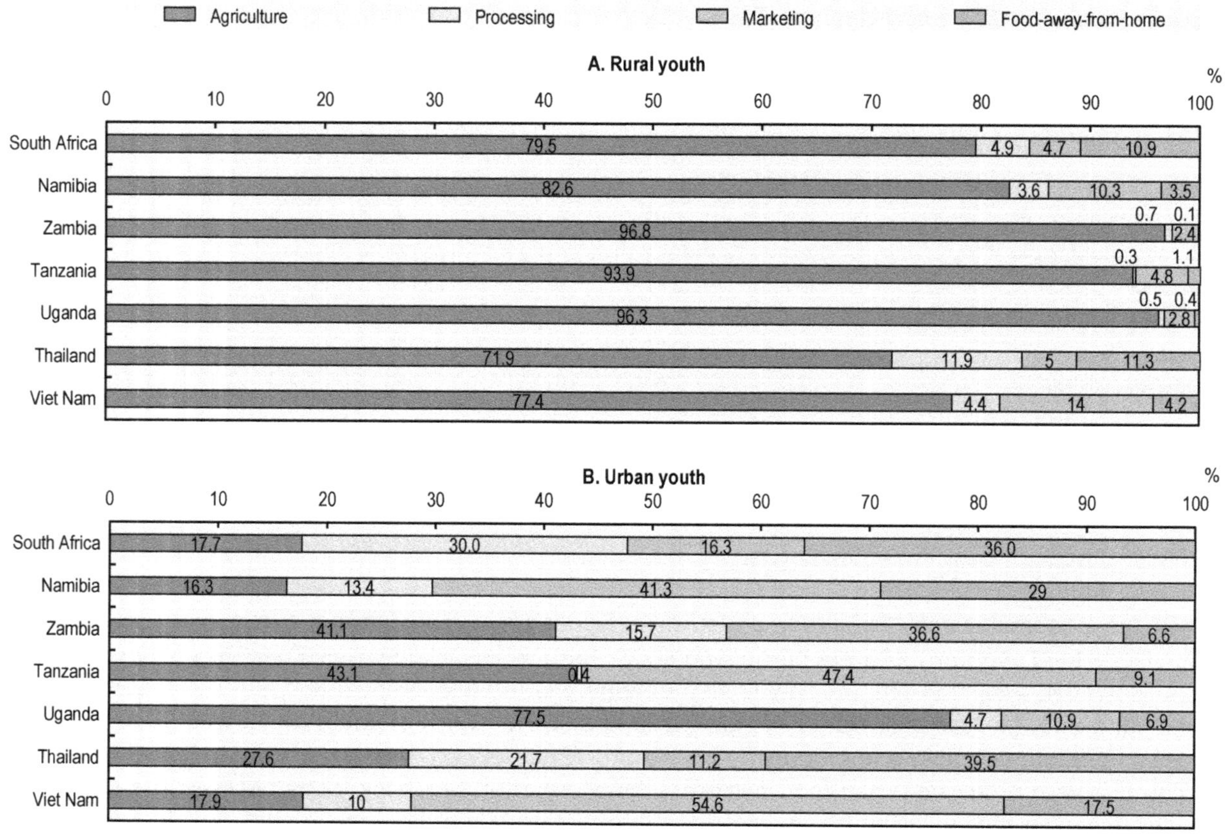

Legend: Agriculture, Processing, Marketing, Food-away-from-home

A. Rural youth (%)

Country	Agriculture	Processing	Marketing	Food-away-from-home
South Africa	79.5	4.9	4.7	10.9
Namibia	82.6	3.6	10.3	3.5
Zambia	96.8	0.7	0.1	2.4
Tanzania	93.9	0.3	1.1	4.8
Uganda	96.3	0.5	0.4	2.8
Thailand	71.9	11.9	5	11.3
Viet Nam	77.4	4.4	14	4.2

B. Urban youth (%)

Country	Agriculture	Processing	Marketing	Food-away-from-home
South Africa	17.7	30.0	16.3	36.0
Namibia	16.3	13.4	41.3	29
Zambia	41.1	15.7	36.6	6.6
Tanzania	43.1	0.4	47.4	9.1
Uganda	77.5	4.7	10.9	6.9
Thailand	27.6	21.7	11.2	39.5
Viet Nam	17.9	10	54.6	17.5

Source: Authors' calculations.

Young women in the food economy

Women play an important role in the food economy, as the majority of food economy jobs are agricultural and women are generally thought to be overrepresented in agricultural work in developing countries (Meinzen-Dick, 2019[8]). Gender norms shape the role women are expected to play in the cultivation, processing and production of food. However, women are not necessarily given the same opportunities as men in agri-food systems or able to use agricultural employment opportunities to achieve economic independence or empowerment. This section assesses how young women fare in the food economy compared to men and adult women and analyses pay gaps and education mismatch in the food economy.

Across all seven countries studied, women participate in the labour force at nearly equal or slightly lesser rates than men. Within the food economy, young women in the lower middle- and low-income African countries (Tanzania, Uganda and Zambia) are just as likely to work in agriculture as young men. In the upper-middle-income African countries (Namibia and South Africa), young women participate in agricultural work at about half the rate of young men (Figure 2.12). In economies where downstream segments are more developed (Namibia, South Africa, Thailand and Viet Nam) more young women than men work in food processing, marketing and food-away-from-home activities, and in particular in the food-away-from-home segment, which includes all services related to food catering (Figure 2.12).

Figure 2.12. Distribution of young men and young women by food economy segment, in selected African and Asian countries

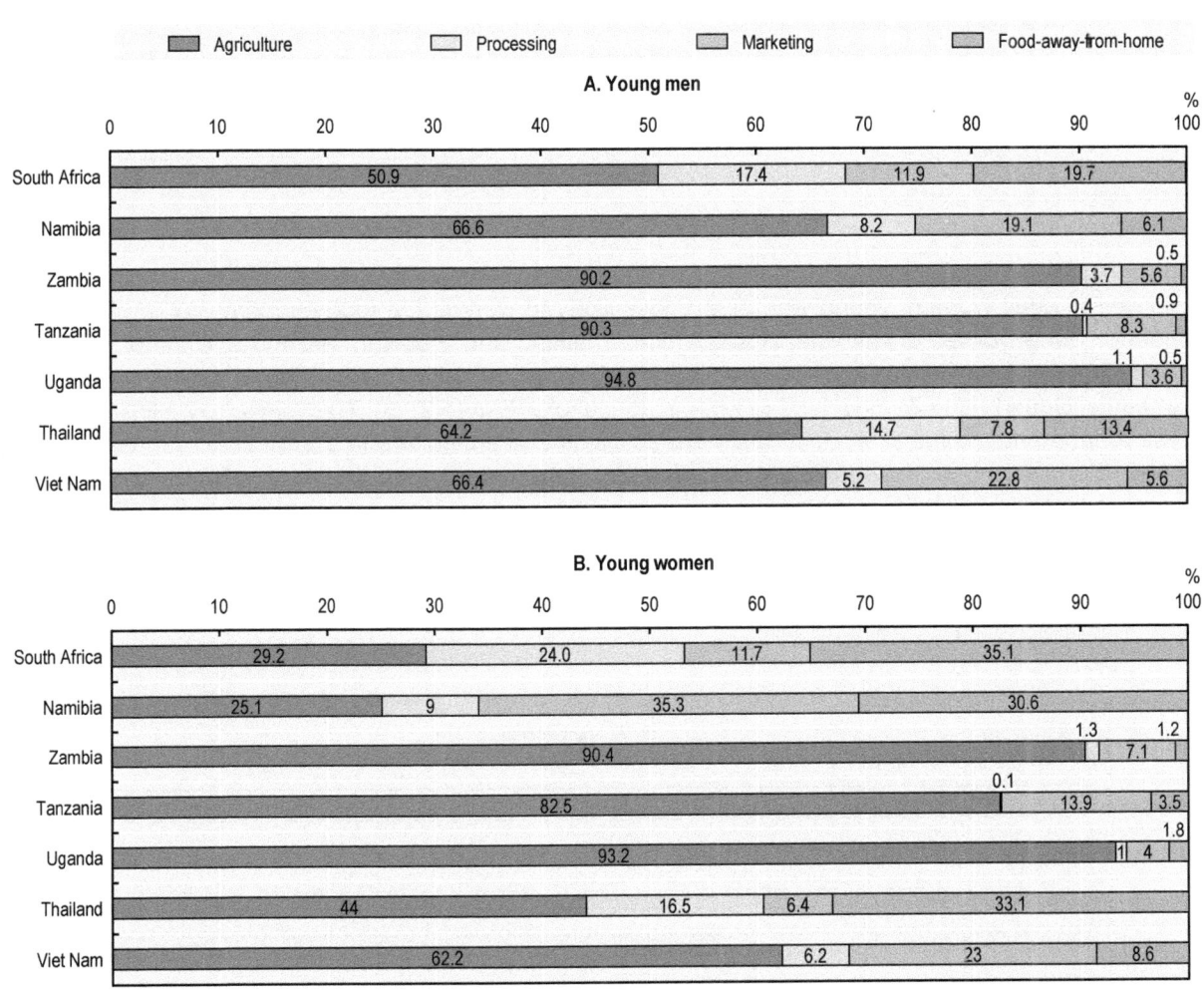

Source: Authors' calculations.

Young women tend to earn less than young men in the food economy, even in sectors where they are meant to be over-represented. In Uganda and Viet Nam, the average median pay gaps are the highest, at 37.5% and 16.6% respectively (Table 2.2). There are still higher gaps by sector: in Uganda, the pay gap for food-away-from-home is 67%, while in Namibia, the youth gender pay gap for food-away-from-home is 39%. By segment, there are exceptions: in South Africa, Tanzania and Thailand, young women earn more in food marketing than young men on average; and in Namibia, Thailand and Uganda, young women in agriculture appear to earn slightly more than young men.

Table 2.2. Median hourly wage of food economy youth by gender and food economy segment, in local currency units, in selected African and Asian countries

		South Africa	Namibia	Tanzania	Uganda	Thailand	Viet Nam
Young men	Total food economy	18.5	5.8	684.3	955.6	40.0	18 269
Young women	Total food economy	18.1	5.9	577.4	592.8	38.8	15 734

Young men	Agriculture	16.9	4.5	684.3	769.8	37.5	17 308
	Processing	20.8	12.7	N/A	1 484.7	38.8	18 619
	Marketing	21.9	8.2	404.2	962.3	46.9	20 769
	Food-away-from-home	20.8	11.2	1 616.6	962.3	42.9	17 752
Young women	Agriculture	15.6	4.9	577.4	1 077.8	38.5	15 071
	Processing	19.5	9.4	N/A	N/A	38.5	15 976
	Marketing	23.6	5.8	1 837.9	513.2	62.5	17 684
	Food-away-from-home	17.2	6.6	N/A	393.1	40.0	11 834

Note: Information not available for Zambia.
Source: Authors' calculations.

Compared to adult women, young women are less likely to work in the food economy. When in the food economy, young women in Namibia, South Africa, Thailand and Viet Nam are more likely to find jobs in the downstream segments, which may be a result of higher educational attainment, while young women in Tanzania, Uganda and Zambia tend to work in agriculture (Figure 2.13). This may also be linked to lower access to land and capital to work in upstream activities and agriculture in a profitable manner, resulting in lower-return activities. For those with higher educational attainment, this may reflect a preference to enter more lucrative off-farm activities.

Figure 2.13. Distribution of food economy jobs held by adult women and young women, by food economy segment, in selected African and Asian countries

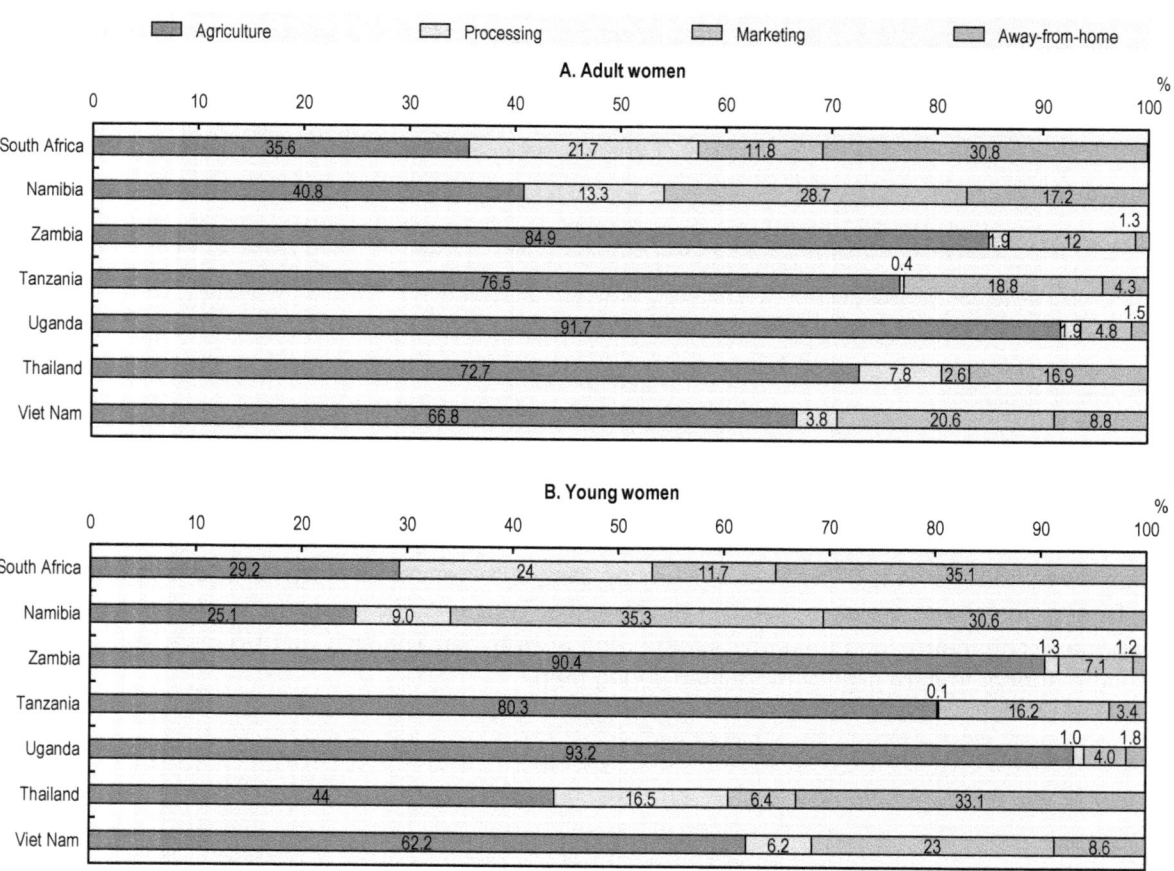

Source: Authors' calculations.

Young women working in the food economy have a lower level of education than women in non-food economy jobs. Young women employed outside of the food economy tend to have at least a secondary level of education (Figure 2.14). On average, 20% of young women employed in non-food economy jobs have a tertiary degree, as opposed to 6% among those in the food economy. Similarly, more young women (52%) employed in non-food economy jobs obtain a secondary level of education, compared to the food economy (46%). This pattern is notable for all the middle-income countries, where a significantly larger share of young women report attending and/or attaining a tertiary level of education.

Figure 2.14. Distribution of young women in the food and non-food economies by educational attainment, in selected African and Asian countries

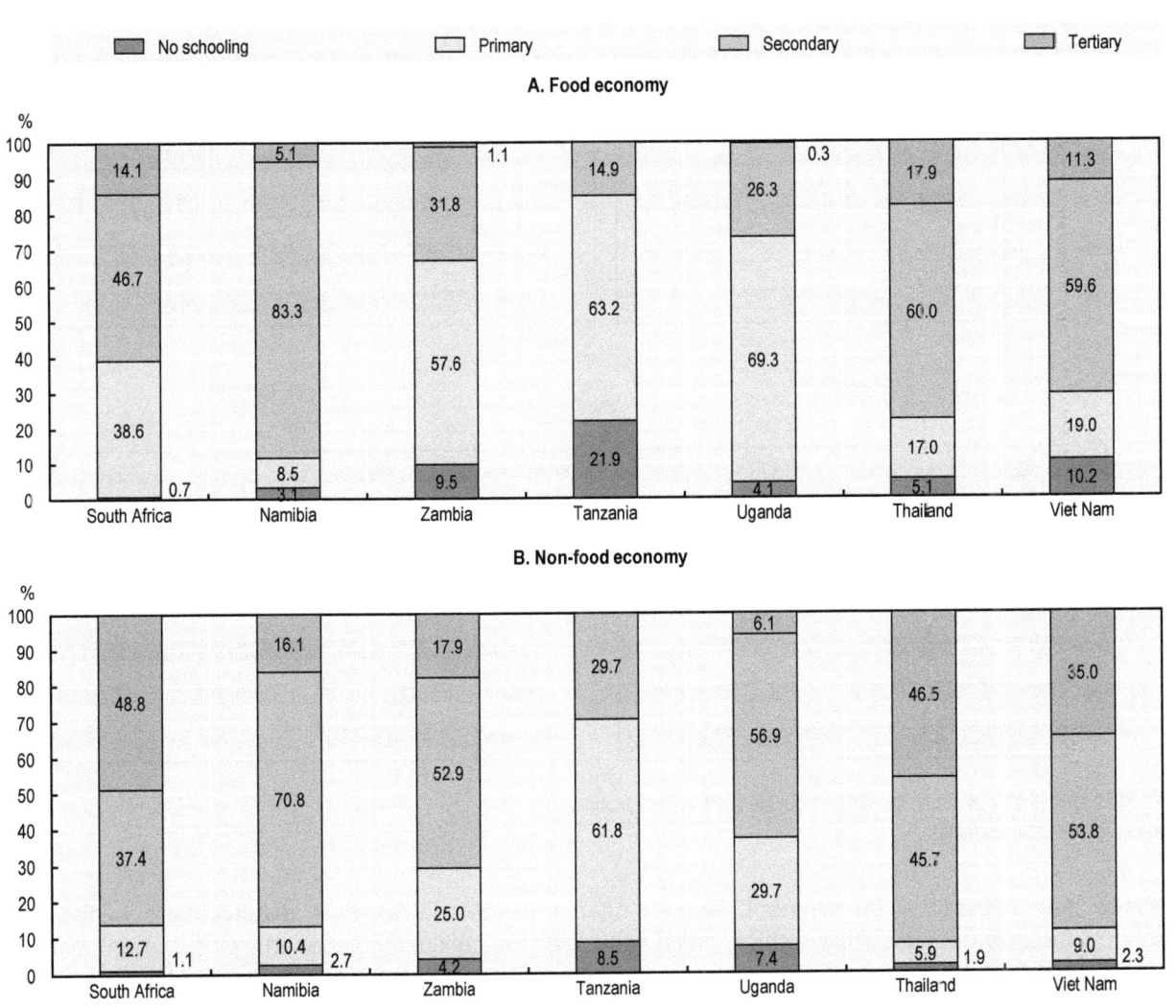

Source: Authors' calculations.

Young women working in downstream segments of the food economy tend to have a higher level of education. A large share of young women working in food processing, food marketing and food-away-from-home segments have a tertiary education. Not surprisingly, young women in the food economy with a primary education or less are more likely to work in the agricultural production segment, but a non-negligible proportion of young women with secondary degrees are also found in agriculture in Tanzania,

Uganda and Zambia, as well as Thailand and Viet Nam, pointing to a large degree of skills mismatch and limited opportunities to move to downstream activities Figure 2.15.

Figure 2.15. Distribution of young women across food economy employment by level of education, in selected African and Asian countries

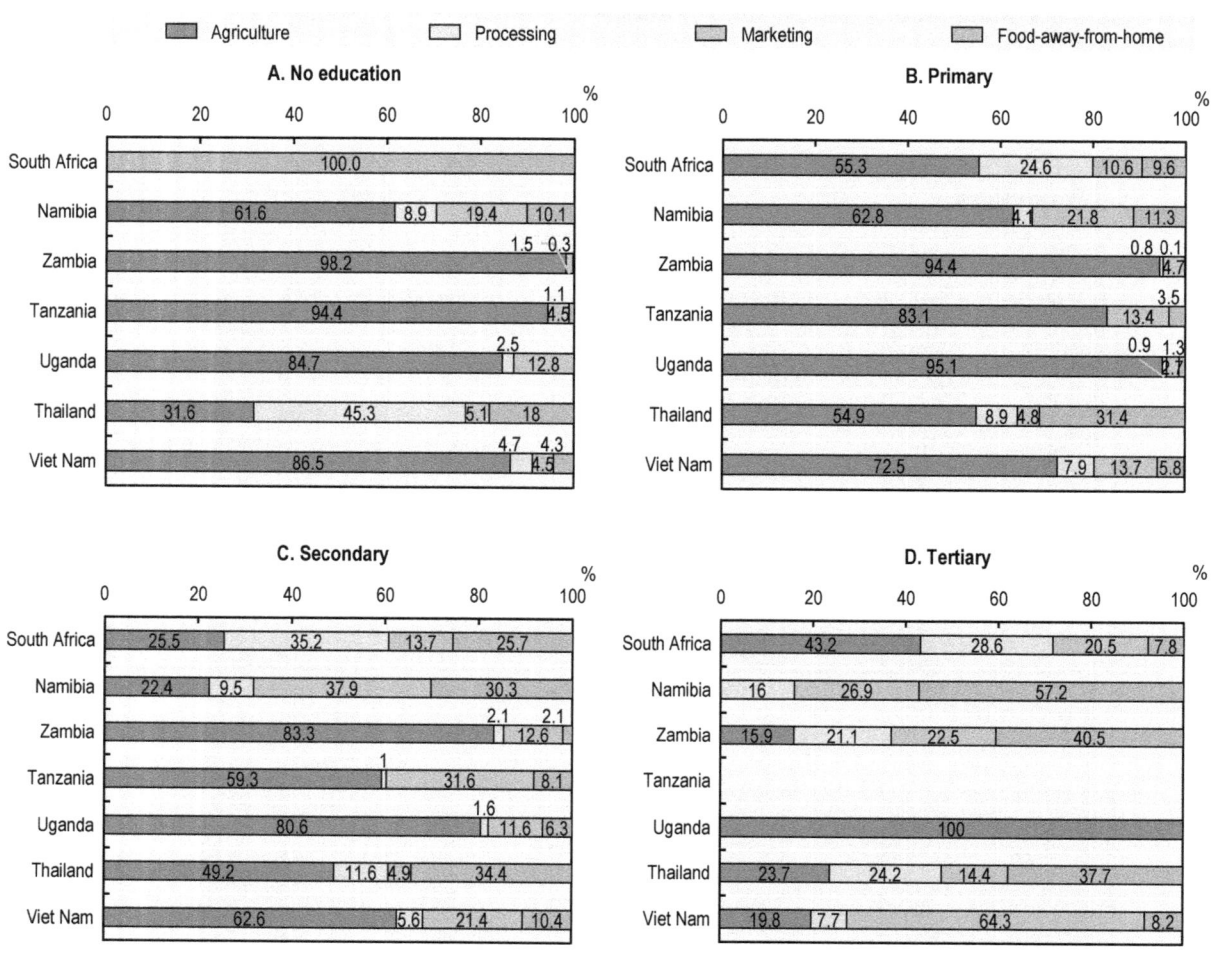

Note: No information is available for tertiary educated women in Tanzania.
Source: Authors' calculations.

Despite their substantial involvement, women often find themselves at a disadvantage in the food economy, notably the agricultural sector, which comprises the bulk of food economy employment, but also in food-away-from-home, where women are most likely to be employed. Women have reduced access to resources, technology, and opportunities in agriculture and rural areas, are paid less than male workers and suffer from reduced agricultural productivity as a result (Doss and SOFA Team, 2011[9]; Quisumbing et al., 1998[10]). The outmigration of men to urban areas and the increasing feminisation of the agricultural sector in sub-Saharan African countries suggest that the productivity of the agricultural sector will continue to be affected by gender inequalities.

COVID-19, youth and the food economy: Focus on South Africa

Lockdown policies adopted during the COVID-19 crisis have represented a serious threat to maintaining food security throughout the world, generating a shock to supply and demand in the agri-food market by disrupting agricultural and food supply chains. Such measures have affected the food economy through 1) reduced employment; 2) reduced production of agricultural goods; 3) increased costs along the agri-food supply chain due to sanitation measures; and 4) cash flow issues due to reduced consumer ability to pay for goods.

Restrictive measures adopted during the COVID-19 crisis have also negatively impacted youth employment, with serious implications for the career trajectories of young people in both developed and developing economies. Youth employment is especially vulnerable to shocks and is expected to be most severely affected by the restrictive measures taken by several countries during the COVID-19 crisis (Schoon and Mann, 2020[11]). Demand for employment falls during a crisis, and employers refrain from training new labour market entrants and other inexperienced workers, impeding successful school-to-work transitions. Previous shocks, such as the global financial crisis of 2008/09, similarly destroyed employment, with youth bearing the brunt of the losses (Cho and Newhouse, 2011[12]).

In South Africa, among food economy workers, youth were the most impacted by the loss of employment in 2020, accounting for more than half of all food economy employment losses. Between Q1 2020 and Q3 2020, 1.7 million net jobs in total employment were lost in South Africa. Of these jobs, 9.2% were held by youth in the food economy, which represented more than half of all overall food economy job losses (15.8%). The majority of youth employment lost between Q3 2019 and Q3 2020 were in agriculture and food services: 50.3% in agricultural production, 1% in manufacturing; 2.6% in trade (retail and wholesale); 16.5% in transport;[1] and 30.7% in food services and food-away-from-home.

Between Q1 2019 and Q1 2020, just over a quarter of a million new jobs were created in the food economy in South Africa. In Q1 2020, 271 813 more jobs than the previous year (Q1 2019) were registered (Figure 2.16). As the year progressed, the impacts of the COVID-19 pandemic led to the near-total loss of these jobs: between Q2 2019 and Q2 2020, 221 055 net food economy jobs were lost, and between Q3 2019 and Q3 2020, 265 711 food economy jobs were lost. Formal food economy employment represented 2.5% of the jobs created between Q1 2019 and Q1 2020 and 78% and 66% of the jobs lost between Q2 2019 and Q2 2020 and Q3 2019 and Q3 2020, respectively.

Figure 2.16. Difference in total employment and total food economy employment between quarters 1 through 3 of 2019 to 2020, in South Africa

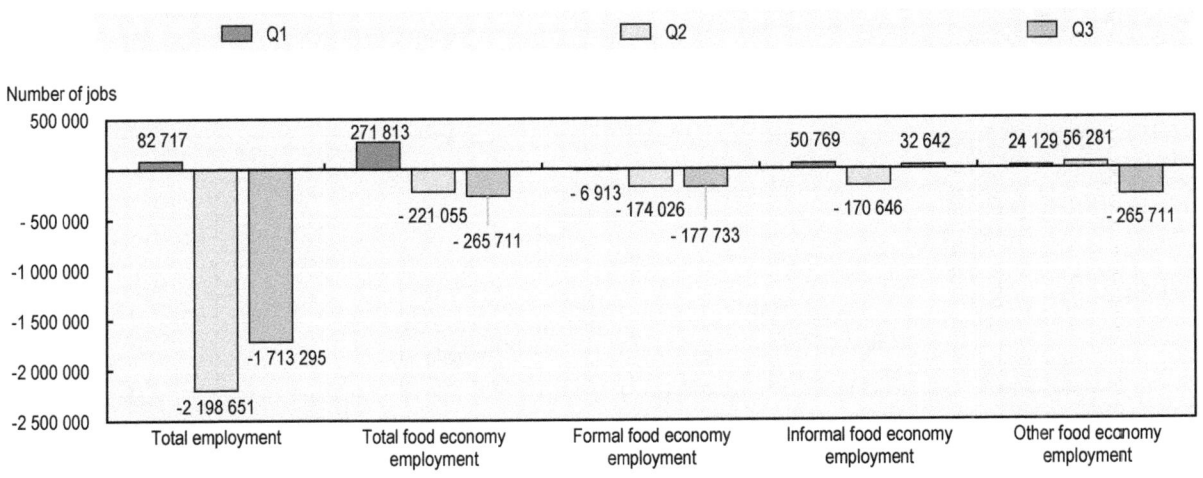

Source: Authors' calculations based on the (2019[13]) and (2020[14]) South Africa Quarterly Labour Force Surveys, Quarters 1 through 3.

Youth food economy employment represented a significant share of the total jobs lost in South Africa between 2019 and 2020, but formal work was more likely to be lost than informal work. Between Q1 2019 and Q1 2020, youth food economy employment represented 58% of all new jobs created in the food economy; 22.6% were formal and 77% informal (Figure 2.17). Between Q2 2019 and Q2 2020, youth food economy jobs represented 64% of the total food economy jobs lost in South Africa, with 65% of these jobs being formal employment and 34% informal employment.

Figure 2.17. Difference in youth food economy employment by informal status between quarters of 2019 to 2020, in South Africa

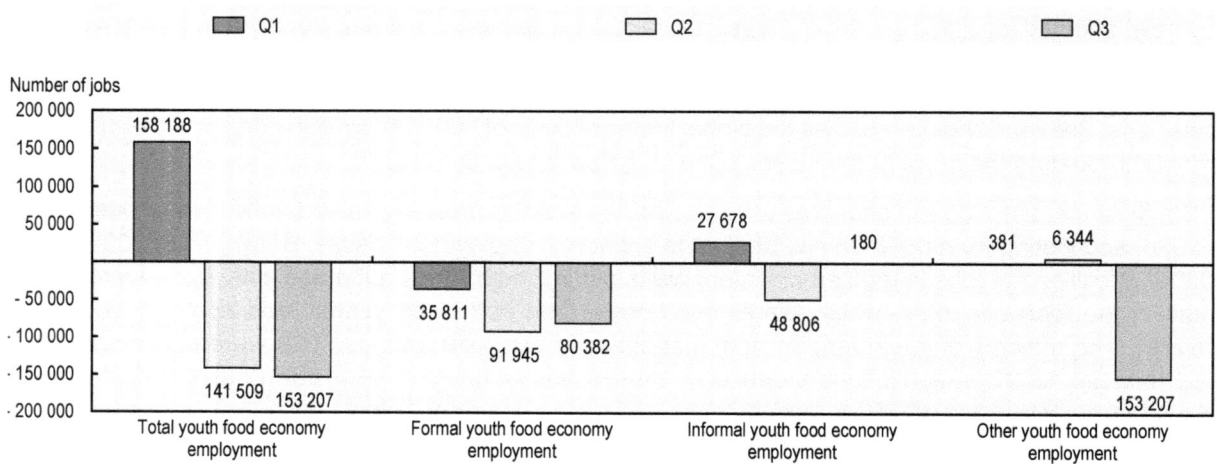

Source: Authors' calculations based on the (2019[13]) and (2020[14]) South Africa Quarterly Labour Force Surveys, Quarters 1 through 3.

South African youth in agriculture, transport and services suffered the largest losses in 2020. Figure 2.18 depicts the gradual loss of jobs for the first three quarters of 2020, as compared to 2019. Agricultural, service and transport jobs held by youth were largely lost by the second and third quarters due to lockdown measures.

Figure 2.18. Difference in youth food economy employment by food economy segment between quarters of 2019 to 2020, in South Africa

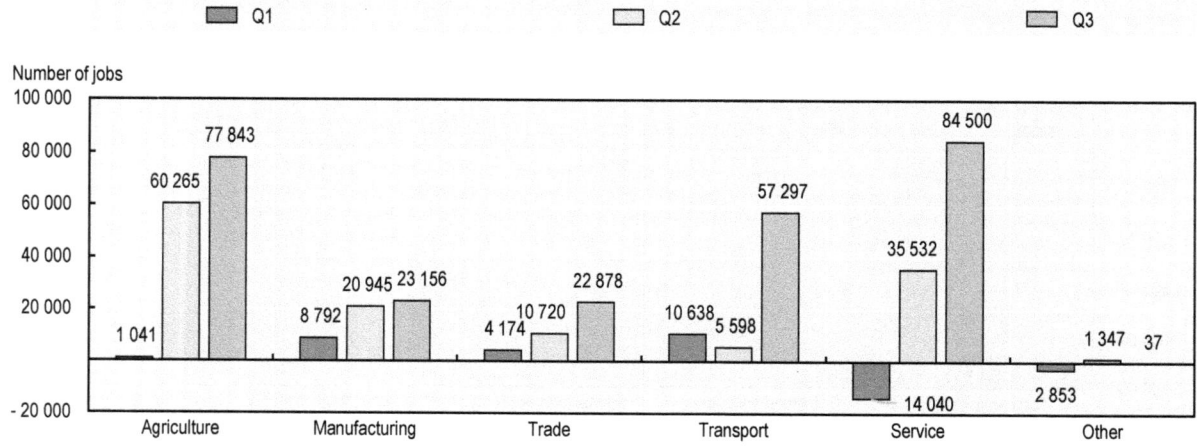

Source: Authors' calculations based on the (2019[13]) and (2020[14]) South Africa Quarterly Labour Force Surveys, Quarters 1 through 3.

Restrictive measures adopted during the COVID-19 crisis have had a disruptive impact on agri-food system production and employment, with the potential to seriously disrupt food security in developing countries. Restrictive measures have halted the regular movement of people and goods within and between territories and disrupted the rhythm and the conditions under which most work could be conducted. Agricultural production has suffered from such labour shortages, and there have been severe implications for the production and supply of food and food-related goods, as well as for the nutritional value of food baskets consumed by households during COVID.

The extreme loss of jobs due to the measures taken during the crisis has affected the livelihoods and revenue streams of households dependent on the food economy and has likely pushed many of these workers into poverty. The World Bank estimated that 119 to 124 million people were likely pushed into extreme poverty as a result of the crisis in 2020 and that the majority of the new poor live in rural areas (Lakner et al., 2021[15]). In addition to poverty, the food security of Africa, notably, is at risk, and the potential to create food supply shortages that will compound the experience of impoverishment will be difficult to handle moving forward (FAO, 2020[16]).

The disruption of food systems negatively impacted youth employment in the food economy, destroying most of the jobs held by young persons in 2020. Serious implications exist for the length and success rate of school-to-work transitions, as prior studies show that economic recessions increase the youth unemployment rate compared to the adult employment rate, while earnings tend to decline after a recession.

Conclusion

For most countries studied, the food economy represents an important share of economic activity and employment for youth. Despite the heterogeneity of food economy employment across sample countries, the majority of food-related activities are still centred in rural areas and around agricultural jobs. Urban food economy employment is much more diversified than in rural areas. The share of non-farm rural agri-food activity is small but non-negligible.

Currently, the majority of food economy jobs do not provide stable or decent employment. For the vast majority of young workers, a food economy job represents their primary economic activity, and, in general, they are paid much less than their peers working in non-food economy sectors, although there are some exceptions by country in food marketing and processing segments.

Young people in the food economy are largely employed in informal and vulnerable forms of work, which provide little employment and income security. Due to the staggering extent of informality in the food economy, many of these youth do not have any social security through their jobs, which affects their ability to weather economic shocks and smooth consumption. In addition, restrictive measures adopted during the COVID-19 crisis have destroyed many jobs, and youth in the food economy have been disproportionately affected, proving again that youth livelihoods are the most at risk during economic downturns. The pandemic has also clearly increased the vulnerability to and the intensity of child labour including for the age group 15-17.

Notes

[1] Not adjusted for food.

References

Allen, A. et al. (2016), *Agrifood Youth Employment and Engagement Study (AgYEES)*, Michigan State University, East Lansing, Michigan. [3]

Allen, T. and P. Heinrigs (2016), *Emerging Opportunities in the West African Food Economy*, OECD Publishing, Paris, https://doi.org/10.1787/5jlvfj4968jb-en. [7]

Allen, T., P. Heinrigs and I. Heo (2018), "Agriculture, Food and Jobs in West Africa", *West African Papers*, No. 14, OECD Publishing, Paris, https://dx.doi.org/10.1787/dc152bc0-en. [1]

Cho, Y. and D. Newhouse (2011), *How Did the Great Recession Affect Different Types of Workers? Evidence from 17 Middle-Income Countries*, World Bank, Washington, DC, http://dx.doi.org/10.1596/1813-9450-5636. [12]

Dolislager, M. et al. (2021), "Youth and Adult Agrifood System Employment in Developing Regions: Rural (Peri-urban to Hinterland) vs. Urban", *Journal of Development Studies*, Vol. 57/4, pp. 571-593, http://dx.doi.org/10.1080/00220388.2020.1808198. [4]

Doss, C. and SOFA Team (2011), "The role of women in agriculture", *ESA Working Papers*, No. 11-02, FAO, http://www.fao.org/economic/esa (accessed on 7 April 2021). [9]

FAO (2020), "COVID-19 and Its Impact on Agri-food Systems, Food Security and Nutrition: Implications and Priorities for the Africa Region", *FAO Regional Conference for Africa*, http://dx.doi.org/10.4060/ca9692en. [16]

Lakner, C. et al. (2021), *Updated estimates of the impact of COVID-19 on global poverty: Looking back at 2020 and the outlook for 2021*, https://blogs.worldbank.org/opendata/updated-estimates-impact-covid-19-global-poverty-looking-back-2020-and-outlook-2021 (accessed on 8 April 2021). [15]

Meinzen-Dick, R. (2019), *Empowering Africa's women farmers*, International Food Policy Research Institute (IFPRI) Blog, https://www.ifpri.org/blog/empowering-africas-women-farmers (accessed on 3 May 2021). [8]

OECD (2017), *Unlocking the Potential of Youth Entrepreneurship in Developing Countries: From Subsistence to Performance*, Development Centre Studies, OECD Publishing, Paris, https://doi.org/10.1787/9789264277830-en. [5]

OECD (2017), *Youth Aspirations and the Reality of Jobs in Developing Countries: Mind the Gap*, Development Centre Studies, OECD Publishing, Paris, http://dx.doi.org/dx.doi.org/10.1787/9789264285668-en. [6]

Quisumbing, A. et al. (1998), "Gender issues for food security in developing countries: Implications for project design and implementation", *Canadian Journal of Development Studies*, Vol. 19/1 Suppl. 1, pp. 185-208, http://dx.doi.org/10.1080/02255189.1998.9669784. [10]

Schoon, I. and A. Mann (2020), "School-to-work transitions during coronavirus: Lessons from the 2008 Global Financial Crisis", *OECD Education and Skills Today*, https://oecdedutoday.com/school-work-during-coronavirus-2008-global-financial-crisis/ (accessed on 29 April 2021). [11]

Statistics South Africa (2020), *Quarterly Labour Force Surveys 2020*, Quarterly Labour Force Surveys. [14]

Statistics South Africa (2019), *Quarterly Labour Force Surveys 2019*, Quarterly Labour Force Surveys. [13]

UN DESA (2019), *2019 Revision of World Population Prospects*, United Nations Department of Economic and Social Affairs, New York, https://population.un.org/wpp/ (accessed on 12 February 2021). [2]

3. Booming demand: A new dawn for local food economies

Over the coming decade, dietary habits will continue to undergo changes resulting in a transformation of the food economy. Key underlying driving factors include a large segment of the populations in Asia and sub-Saharan Africa obtaining "global middle-class" status and a rapid urbanisation process in both regions. These trends will likely increase demand for processed and higher-quality food products. Based on a uniquely disaggregated dataset on sectoral employment, this chapter provides a forecast of the potential employment growth in the food economy at horizon 2030 for a set of 11 sub-Saharan African countries, as well as 2 countries in Southeast Asia.

The long-term prospects of the food economy are influenced by income growth and urbanisation. Income growth in low- and middle-income countries across sub-Saharan Africa and Southeast Asia is indeed likely to hasten the transition towards higher calorie intakes and consumption of processed food (OECD-FAO, 2020[1]; Tschirley et al., 2015[2]; Worku et al., 2017[3]). Similarly, rapid urbanisation and population growth create new dietary habits and higher demand for agriculture inputs and food-related services such as restaurants and catering, which is expected to transform the downstream segments of the food economy in processing and create new employment for rural and urban youth (Hussein and Suttie, 2016[4]; Berdegué and Proctor, 2014[5]). However, urbanisation in developing countries also presents a series of challenges for the food economy, as urban areas sprawl with low density (especially small and medium-sized cities) and increasingly encroach on fertile land and reduce the scope for food production in peri-urban and surrounding rural areas (Cabannes and Marocchino, 2018[6]).

An important question, therefore, is to what extent such trends could translate into more and better jobs in the food economy, especially for youth. The answer clearly depends on the extent to which local food systems will take up the challenge of higher and changing domestic demand for food, and, if so, which type of local agri-food systems will emerge.

To start looking at this complex question, it is useful first to investigate what could be the employment growth potential in the food economy directly associated with income growth and urbanisation in the next decade, holding all else constant and assuming no change in policy directions and agri-food models. This chapter presents the results of a forecasting exercise, showing how urbanisation trends and the emergence of the middle-class in Asia and Africa could affect employment growth at horizon 2030.

The analysis is undertaken for the seven countries discussed in Chapter 1, as well as for six additional sub-Saharan African countries, and for the four sub-sectors of the food economy: food agriculture, food processing, food marketing and food-away-from-home. The 13 countries therefore are Côte d'Ivoire, Ghana, Mali, Namibia, Niger, Nigeria, Senegal, South Africa, Tanzania, Thailand, Uganda, Viet Nam and Zambia.

The emergence of a "global middle class" and rapid urbanisation

Income growth in low- and middle-income countries across sub-Saharan Africa and Southeast Asia is likely to increase demand for food products and services in both quantitative and qualitative terms. Key underlying trends consist in the accession of large segments of populations in Asia and sub-Saharan Africa to the "global middle-class" status, as well as, relatedly, a rapid urbanisation process. The number of people belonging to the global middle class is projected to increase by 44% between now and 2030. The "global middle class" is often defined as individuals living with USD 10-100 per capita per day, in purchasing power parity, expressed in 2005 dollars (Kharas, 2010[7]; Kharas, 2017[8]). According to a projection established prior to the global pandemic, the number of people belonging to this category is expected to grow from 3.8 billion in 2020 to 5.4 billion in 2030 (Kharas, 2017[8]). Asia-Pacific and sub-Saharan Africa are the regions with the largest percentage increases of the number of people belonging to this category, with 61% and 73% increases, respectively (see Figure 3.1 and Figure 3.2).

Figure 3.1. Projected number of individuals belonging to the global middle class at horizon 2030, by region, relative to the 2020 level

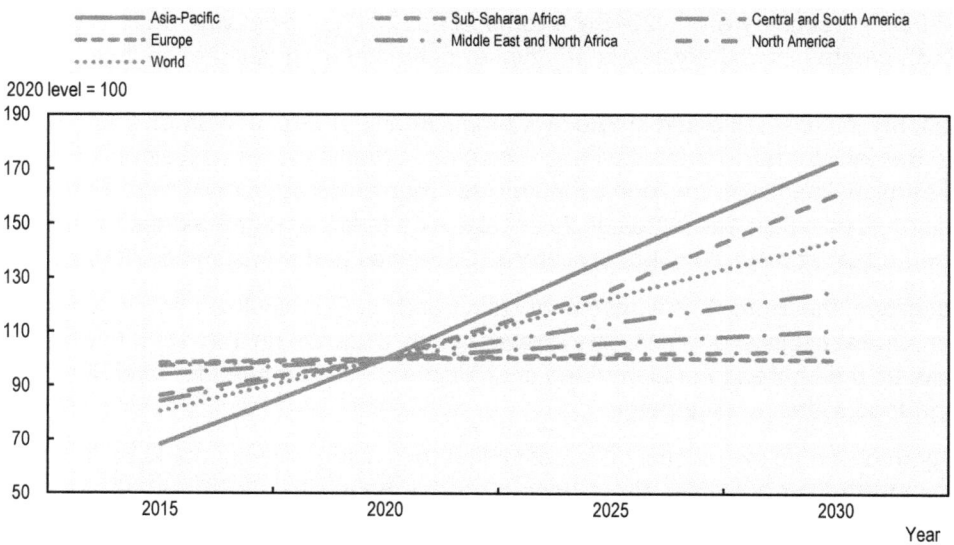

Source: Authors' calculations based on Kharas (2017[8]), *The unprecedented expansion of the global middle class: An update*, https://www.brookings.edu/research/the-unprecedented-expansion-of-the-global-middle-class-2/.

Figure 3.2. Projected share of the population belonging to the global middle class at horizon 2030, by region

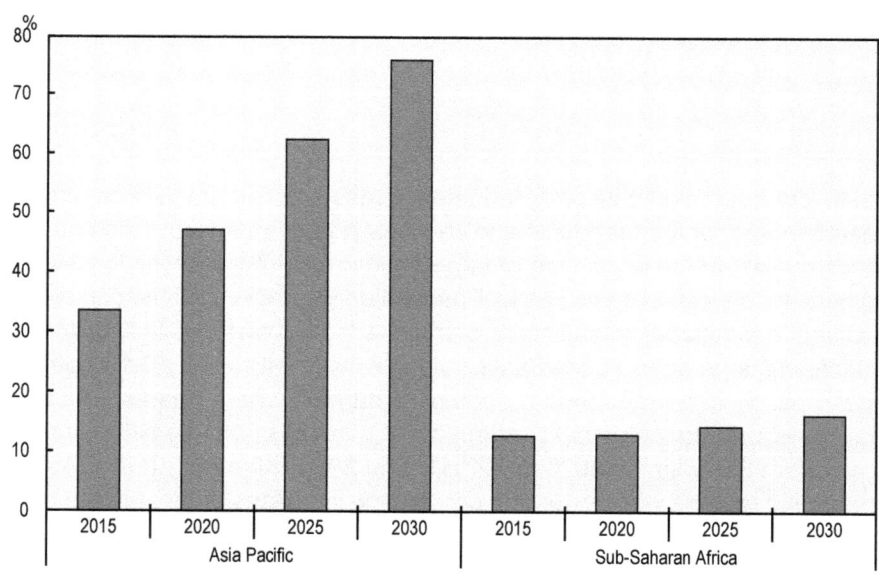

Source: Authors' calculations based on Kharas (2017[8]), The unprecedented expansion of the global middle class: An update, https://www.brookings.edu/research/the-unprecedented-expansion-of-the-global-middle-class-2/.

Middle-class status is strongly associated with increased spending on quality food products and services. In Thailand, middle-class households spend about three times more on restaurants than poorer households (earning less than ten dollars in purchasing power parity per capita per day). In urban areas, the ratio is approximately four to one. In Viet Nam, middle-class households typically spend twice as much on restaurants as poorer households (Figure 3.3).

Figure 3.3. Spending on food-away-from-home in Thailand and Viet Nam, by income class and urban/rural status

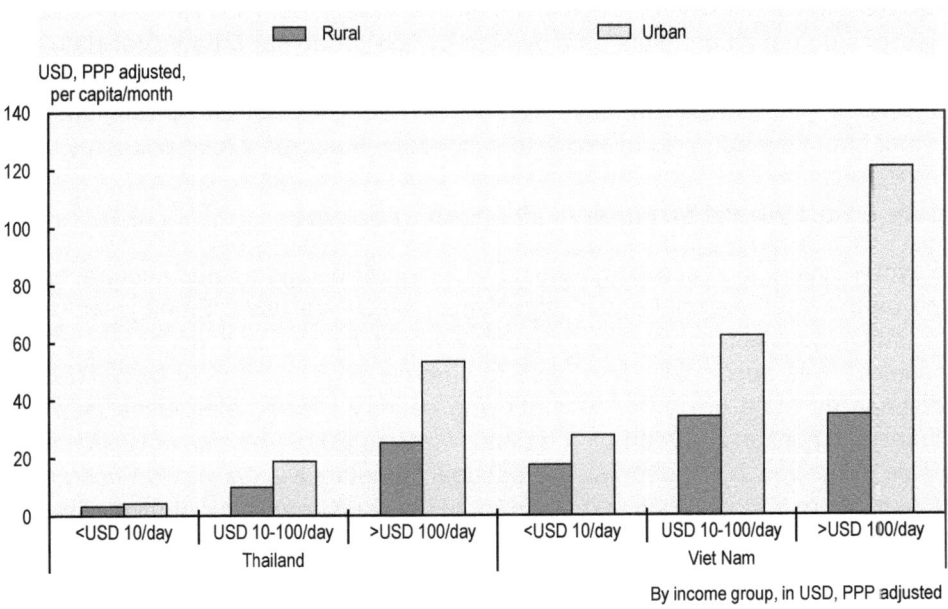

By income group, in USD, PPP adjusted

Note: Income groups are based on total household income divided by the number of family members.
Sources: Authors' calculations based on Socio-Economic Survey (2017) for Thailand, Household Living Standards Survey (2014) for Viet Nam. Purchasing power parity (PPP) conversion factors for private consumption (local currency unit per international dollar) are obtained from the International Comparison Program, World Bank.

Restrictive measures adopted in several countries during the COVID-19 crisis are considerably deteriorating income dynamics. Sixty million additional people could be pushed into poverty in the short term (Lakner et al., 2021[9]), and many economies are expected to exhibit a gross domestic product (GDP) around 5% lower in 2022 than before the crisis (OECD, 2020[10]). While the long-term economic consequences of the crisis are difficult to foresee, one might however expect that at horizon 2030 many of its effects will have dissipated and countries will have converged towards their pre-pandemic trends.

Globally, 55% of the world's population lived in urban areas in 2018, and, by 2050, this share is projected to increase to 68%. In Africa, the majority of the population is still rural with 41% living in urban areas, while Asia became mostly urban for the first time in history in 2019, with more than 50% of its population living in cities (UN DESA, 2019[11]). The urban population in Asia is expected to rise to more than 2.8 billion in 2030, making up 65% of the total population (UN DESA, 2019[11]). In Southeast Asia, the urban population will grow by another 100 million people by 2030, rising from 280 million people today to 373 million, reaching an urbanisation rate of 57% (Florida and Fasche, 2017[12]).

Urbanisation affects dietary habits. Higher urban wages tend to increase the opportunity costs of cooking for personal household consumption. This in turn increases demand for labour-intensive food services, such as restaurants (FAO, 2017[13]). Such services also typically enjoy economic benefits from larger urban markets. These patterns are likely to drive demand for higher-quality food products and services, as well as higher caloric intake per capita over the next decade. Asia-Pacific and Africa are the two regions exhibiting the largest projected rise in caloric intake per capita at horizon 2029 (OECD-FAO, 2020[1]), with increases of 5.9% and 2.7%, respectively.

Employment forecast in the food economy

This section turns to an analysis of the expected changes in employment in the food economy at horizon 2030 related to urbanisation and the emergence of the middle class in Asia and Africa discussed above. While these projections do not differentiate employment by age group nor urban/rural status, they are indicative of opportunities for youth and particularly rural youth. They suggest an overall increase in the absolute number of jobs in the food economy in the countries of interest and a rebalancing of food economy employment from the agricultural sector to secondary and tertiary food economy activities.

Aggregate employment forecast in the food economy

To forecast employment in the food economy, two novel, uniquely disaggregated sectoral employment datasets provided by the International Labour Organization (ILO) are used: Employment by sex and economic activity (ILO modelled estimates) and Employment by sex and economic activity (ISIC level 2). A methodology was specifically developed to harness information from both datasets, using GDP and urbanisation as main predictors and deriving country-specific elasticities (see Annex A). Employment estimates at horizon 2030 rely on the United Nations' *2018 Revision of World Urbanisation Prospects* (available at horizon 2030) and the International Monetary Fund's *World Economic Outlook* GDP forecasts (available at horizon 2025, extended to 2030; see Annex A for details). This approach based on rich longitudinal data represents a considerable improvement over previous food economy employment projections, which relied on a cross-section of observations and strong assumptions on future relationships between food demand and labour market outcomes (Tschirley et al., 2015[2]).

The changing structure of employment in the food economy

For the 11 sub-Saharan African economies studied here, aggregate employment in food agriculture is projected to increase to 86 million jobs in 2030 from 74 million in 2019, a 17% increase. The number of jobs in the downstream segments of the food economy, defined as the sum of food processing, food marketing and food-away-from-home, is also set to increase from 21 million to 29 million in the same period (Figure 3.4). Out of total employment, the share of food economy jobs in 2030 should remain more or less stagnant at around 60%, with the share of jobs in the agriculture segment decreasing slightly from 46% to 44% on average over the 2019-30 period. The share of employment in downstream segments will increase slightly to make up 15% of total employment in 2030 (Figure 3.5).

For the same period regarding the two Southeast Asian economies, the total number of jobs in the food economy will remain stagnant in Thailand and increase slightly in Viet Nam (Figure 3.4). Out of total employment, the food economy is projected to account for over half of the jobs in Thailand and 65% in Viet Nam. The overall share of food economy jobs will decline in both countries, by 4 percentage points in Thailand and 2 percentage points in Viet Nam in 2030, mostly led by a decrease in the share of jobs in the agriculture segment. On the other hand, the share of jobs in downstream activities out of total employment should increase in both Thailand and Viet Nam, by 3 and 4 percentage points, respectively (Figure 3.5).

Figure 3.4. Employment in the food economy, number of jobs, 2019 and 2030

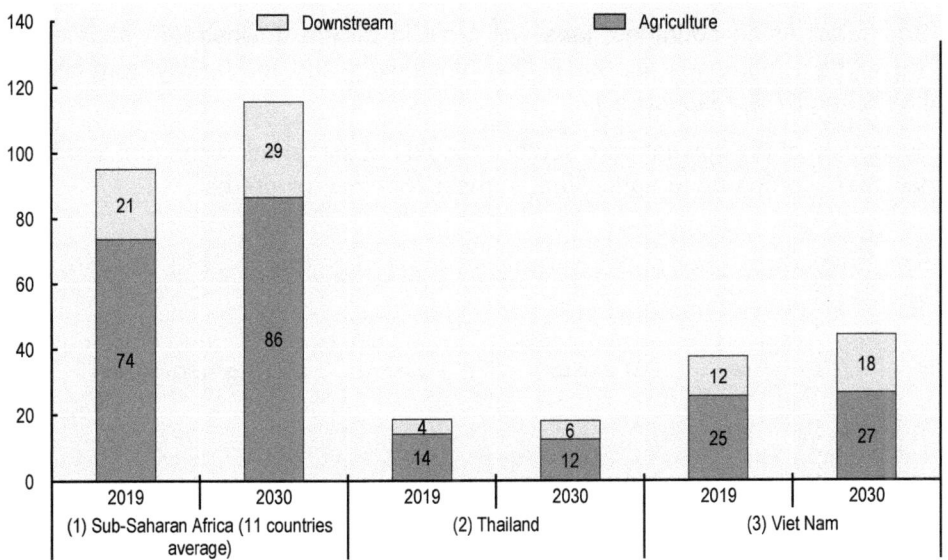

Note: The 11 sub-Saharan African countries include Côte d'Ivoire, Ghana, Mali, Namibia, Niger, Nigeria, Senegal, South Africa, Tanzania, Uganda and Zambia.
Source: Authors' own calculations.

Figure 3.5. Employment in the food economy, share of total employment, 2019 and 2030

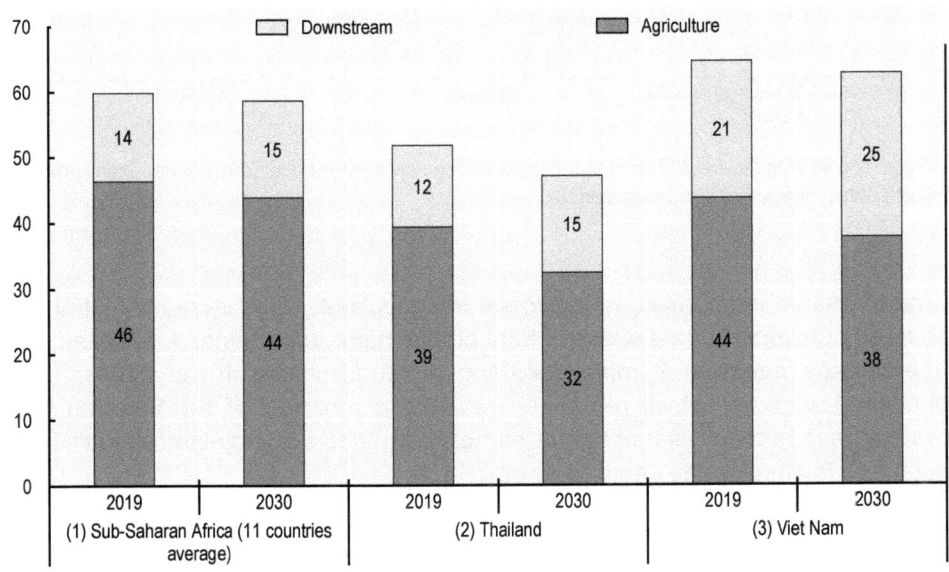

Note: The 11 sub-Saharan African countries include Côte d'Ivoire, Ghana, Mali, Namibia, Niger, Nigeria, Senegal, South Africa, Tanzania, Uganda and Zambia.
Source: Authors' own calculations.

Within the downstream segments of the sub-Saharan African countries, processing will account for 4.9 million jobs in 2030, a 21% increase from 2019, and marketing 21 million jobs, a 39% increase.

JOBS FOR RURAL YOUTH © OECD 2021

Finally, food away-from-home will experience the highest employment increase at 43%, with 4.6 million jobs (Figure 3.6).

In the two Southeast Asian countries, jobs will grow in all the downstream segments of the food economy. The highest increases will be in the processing and food-away-from-home activities in Viet Nam, at 54% and 57%, respectively.

The overall dynamism of the downstream sectors should not overshadow the fact that they start from a relatively small base, compared to agriculture, in most countries of interest.

Figure 3.6. Employment by food economy sector, projected change 2019-30, percentage change over initial level

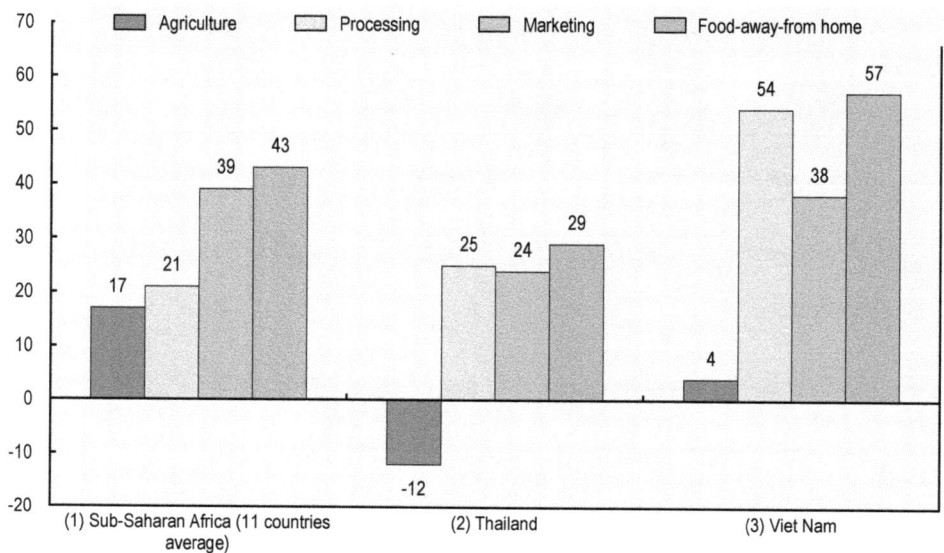

Note: The regional figure is a weighted average. The 11 sub-Saharan African countries include Côte d'Ivoire, Ghana, Mali, Namibia, Niger, Nigeria, Senegal, South Africa, Tanzania, Uganda and Zambia.
Source: Authors' own calculations.

In the sub-Saharan African economies, employment in agriculture, while increasing in absolute terms, should decline nearly universally as a share of total employment, representing, for example, a decline of nearly 20 percentage points in Zambia, following a trend initiated in the 2000s. Despite these dynamics, agricultural employment will remain an essential component of sub-Saharan African labour markets across the next decade, as 8 of the 11 sample countries are projected to maintain more than 40% of their total employment in the sector (Figure 3.7).

Figure 3.7. Employment in agriculture, share of total employment, 2019 and 2030, by country

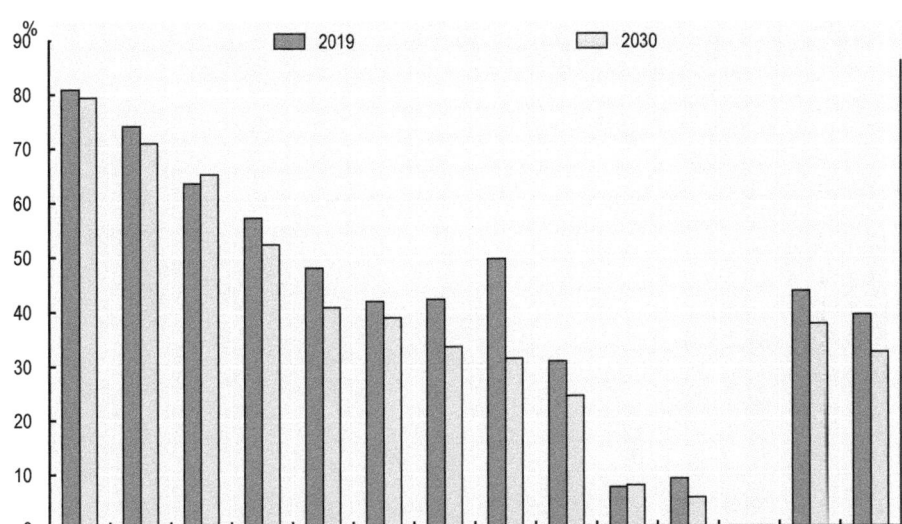

Note: The 11 sub-Saharan African countries include Côte d'Ivoire, Ghana, Mali, Namibia, Niger, Nigeria, Senegal, South Africa, Tanzania, Uganda and Zambia.
Source: Authors' own calculations.

Evolution of the downstream sectors of the food economy

At horizon 2030, the share of employment in the downstream part of the food economy in sub-Saharan Africa will range from 21% of total employment in Nigeria to 4% in Uganda. Employment in downstream sectors should rise most, as a share of total employment, in Zambia (+5 percentage points) and Tanzania (+4 pp). It will decline as a share of total employment only in South Africa and Uganda (>-1 pp). While in the case of Uganda this relative decline is related to quickly increasing overall employment in the rest of the economy, in the case of South Africa an absolute decline in food processing is projected. The trend is in line with the "premature deindustrialisation" of the country since the late 2000s (Imbs, 2013[14]), which is attributed to the rise in extractive activities aimed at exports to emerging Asia, originally triggered by a surge in mineral commodity prices. The trend is rather specific to the country, as middle- and high-income economies tend, in certain circumstances, de-industrialise generally to move into services, while in the case of South Africa the move is towards the primary sector (Imbs, 2013[14]).

Downstream segment employment should increase sharply in Viet Nam (+4 percentage points) and Thailand (+2 percentage points), therefore expanding the trend of a fast modernisation of the food economy which has prevailed over the last two decades in Southeast Asia (Briones, 2019[15]). This dynamic has greatly benefited from the region's investment in transportation infrastructure facilitating rural-urban linkages (Reardon and Timmer, 2014[16]).

Figure 3.8. Employment in downstream sectors of the food economy, share of total employment, 2019 and 2030

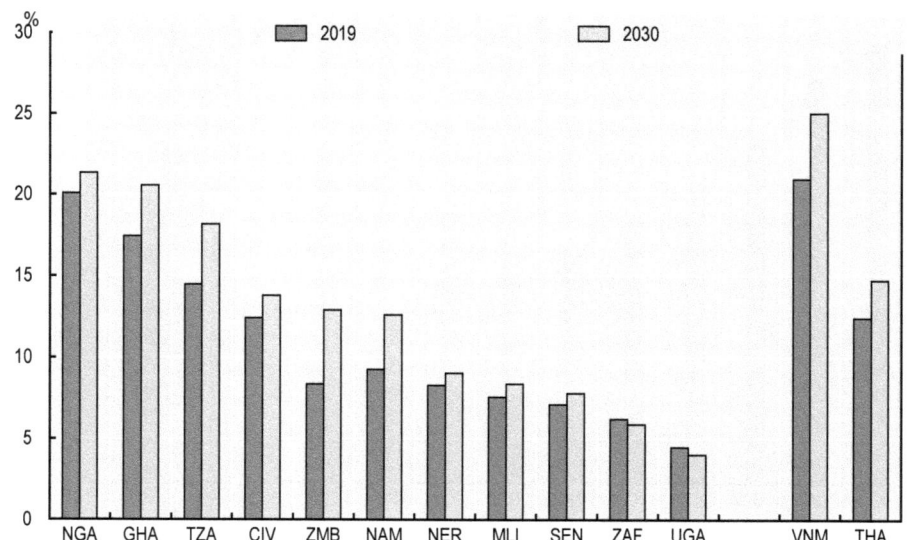

Note: The 11 sub-Saharan African countries include Côte d'Ivoire, Ghana, Mali, Namibia, Niger, Nigeria, Senegal, South Africa, Tanzania, Uganda and Zambia.
Source: Authors' own calculations.

Food processing

As shown in Figure 3.9, food processing employment in sub-Saharan Africa is expected to be highest in Nigeria and lowest in Tanzania (<1%) at horizon 2030. The increase, in terms of share, will be highest in Namibia (+1 percentage point). Five African countries will likely reduce their share of employment in processing over 2019-30, with South Africa experiencing the largest drop (0.4 percentage points), which can be attributed to the deindustrialisation dynamics at play in the country described above.

Thailand and Viet Nam exhibit among the highest shares of total employment in food processing (5% and 4%, respectively) and the fastest expanding ones (+0.6 and +0.8 percentage points, respectively).

Figure 3.9. Employment in food processing, shares of total employment, 2019 and 2030

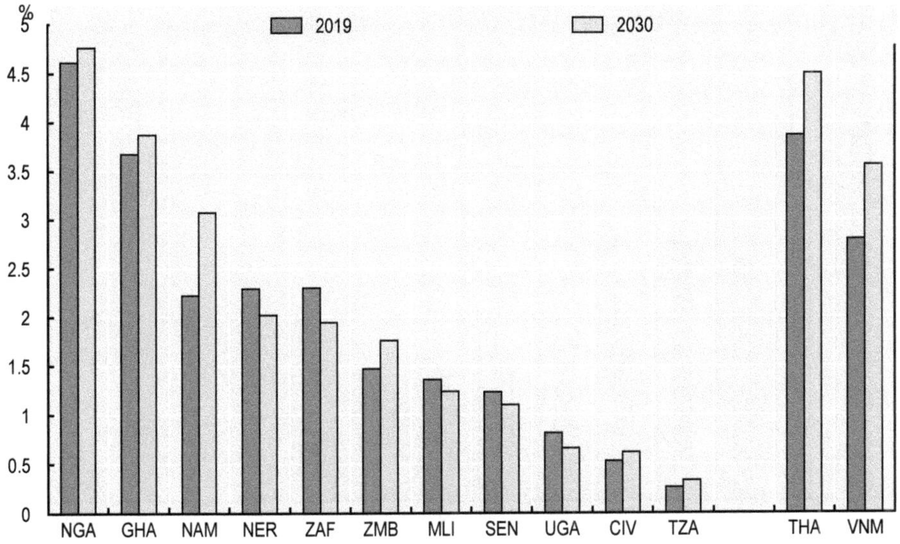

Note: The 11 sub-Saharan African countries include Côte d'Ivoire, Ghana, Mali, Namibia, Niger, Nigeria, Senegal, South Africa, Tanzania, Uganda and Zambia.
Source: Authors' own calculations.

Food marketing

In sub-Saharan Africa, the rise in food marketing employment, consisting of wholesale agricultural machinery, food and beverage retail, and food transport, is projected to be highest in Nigeria (15%) and lowest in South Africa (1%). The sector displays among the highest expected gains in the overall food economy, with namely Zambia and Tanzania exhibiting gains corresponding to more than 4 and 3 percentage points of total employment, respectively. The sector will be virtually stable in South Africa and Uganda.

The sector exhibits heterogeneous patterns among the Southeast Asian sample, as it is projected to represent 15% of employment in Viet Nam but only 2% in Thailand at horizon 2030.

Figure 3.10. Employment in food marketing, shares of total employment, 2019 and 2030

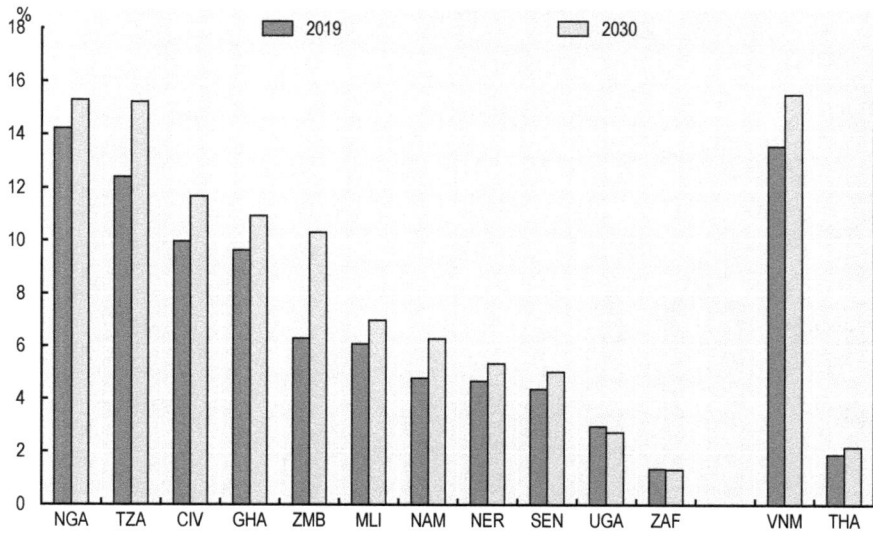

Note: The 11 sub-Saharan African countries include Côte d'Ivoire, Ghana, Mali, Namibia, Niger, Nigeria, Senegal, South Africa, Tanzania, Uganda and Zambia.
Source: Authors' own calculations.

Food-away-from-home

Food-away-from-home is set to represent a large share of total employment by 2030, in particular in Ghana (6%) and Namibia (3%) among sub-Saharan African economies. The sector should gain more than 0.5 percentage points in terms of employment share in Ghana, Namibia and Tanzania. It will experience relative declines in Côte d'Ivoire and Uganda. The Southeast Asian sample countries will enjoy the highest increase in shares, reaching 8% in Thailand and 6% in Viet Nam by 2030.

Figure 3.11. Employment in food-away-from-home, shares of total employment, 2019 and 2030

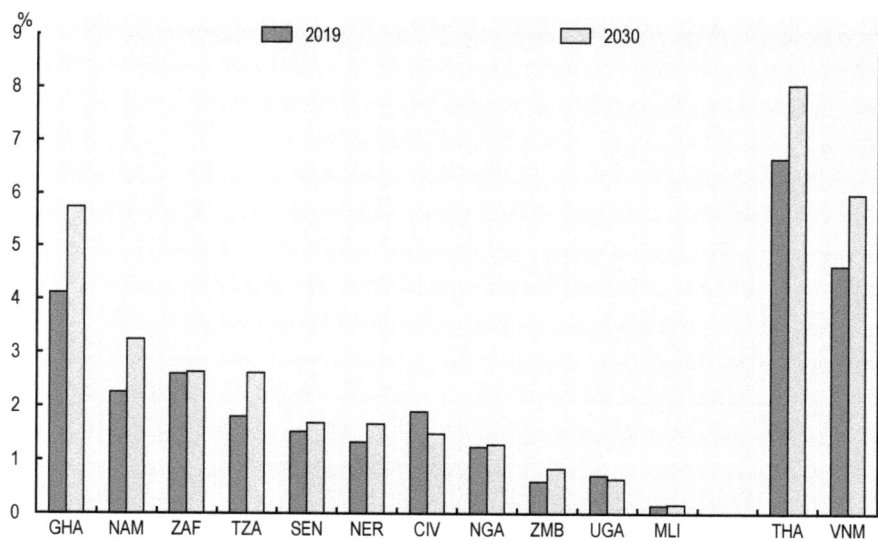

Note: The 11 sub-Saharan African countries include Côte d'Ivoire, Ghana, Mali, Namibia, Niger, Nigeria, Senegal, South Africa, Tanzania, Uganda and Zambia.
Source: Authors' own calculations.

Within the downstream segments, food marketing represents the largest share of total agri-food downstream employment creation in sub-Saharan Africa. The picture is somewhat more balanced in the Southeast Asian countries.

Figure 3.12. Contribution of each downstream sector to overall downstream employment creation, 2019-30

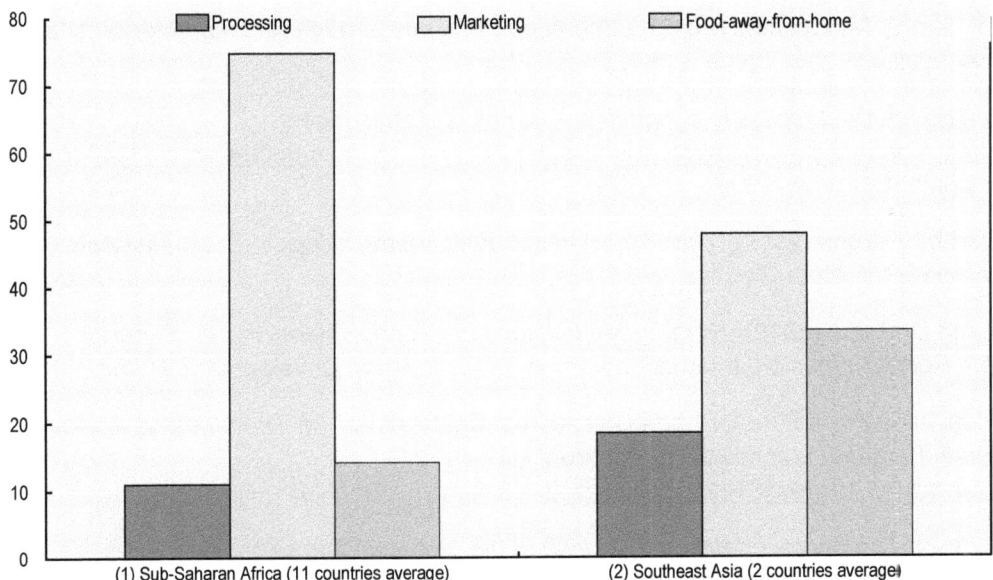

Note: Regional figures are weighted average. The 11 sub-Saharan African countries include Côte d'Ivoire, Ghana, Mali, Namibia, Niger, Nigeria, Senegal, South Africa, Tanzania, Uganda and Zambia.
Source: Authors' own calculations.

Conclusion

This chapter sought to contribute to our understanding of the employment potential in the food economy by forecasting the changes in employment directly associated with rapid urbanisation and the rise of the middle class, holding all else constant. The projections show that such trends would increase the overall level of employment in the food economy, in absolute terms in the case of agriculture and, in the case of downstream segments, in both absolute and relative terms. Looking at the changes within the different segments of the food economy further shows a rebalancing of food economy employment from the agricultural sector to secondary and tertiary food economy activities.

Yet, these results only present a low estimate of the employment growth potential in the food economy, as they assume no change in food models and relate only to rapid urbanisation and the rise of the middle class. The next chapter will discuss how different types of local food systems could further influence the quantity and quality of employment in the food economy beyond urbanisation and rising incomes, while responding to the social, economic and environmental challenges.

References

Berdegué, J. and F. Proctor (2014), *Inclusive Rural–Urban Linkages*, Latin American Center for Rural Development, Santiago. [5]

Briones, R. (2019), "Investing in Rural Youth in the Asia and the Pacific Region", *SSRN Electronic Journal*, http://dx.doi.org/10.2139/ssrn.3532483. [15]

Cabannes, Y. and C. Marocchino (2018), *Integrating Food into Urban Planning*, International Fund for Agricultural Development, UCL Press, Rome. [6]

FAO (2017), *The future of food and agriculture –Trends and challenges*, http://www.fao.org/policy-support/tools-and-publications/resources-details/en/c/472484/ (accessed on 1 February 2021). [13]

Florida, R. and M. Fasche (2017), *The Rise of the Urban Creative Class in Southeast Asia*, Martin Prosperity Institute, Toronto. [12]

Hussein, K. and D. Suttie (2016), *Rural-urban linkages and food systems in sub-Saharan Africa: The Rural Dimension*, International Fund for Agricultural Development, Rome. [4]

Imbs, J. (2013), "The Premature Deindustrialization of South Africa", in *The Industrial Policy Revolution II*, Palgrave Macmillan UK, London, http://dx.doi.org/10.1057/9781137335234_20. [14]

Kharas, H. (2017), *The unprecedented expansion of the global middle class: An update*, Brookings Institution, https://www.brookings.edu/research/the-unprecedented-expansion-of-the-global-middle-class-2/ (accessed on 5 July 2021). [8]

Kharas, H. (2010), "The Emerging Middle Class in Developing Countries", *OECD Development Centre Working Papers*, No. 285, OECD Publishing, Paris, https://dx.doi.org/10.1787/5kmmp8lncrns-en. [7]

Lakner, C. et al. (2021), *Updated estimates of the impact of COVID-19 on global poverty: Looking back at 2020 and the outlook for 2021*, https://blogs.worldbank.org/opendata/updated-estimates-impact-covid-19-global-poverty-looking-back-2020-and-outlook-2021 (accessed on 8 April 2021). [9]

OECD (2020), *OECD Economic Outlook, Volume 2020 Issue 1*, OECD Publishing, Paris, https://dx.doi.org/10.1787/0d1d1e2e-en. [10]

OECD-FAO (2020), *Agricultural Outlook 2020-2029*, https://www.oecd-ilibrary.org/agriculture-and-food/oecd-fao-agricultural-outlook-2020-2029_1112c23b-en (accessed on 5 July 2021). [1]

Reardon, T. and C. Timmer (2014), "Five inter-linked transformations in the Asian agrifood economy: Food security implications", *Global Food Security*, Vol. 3/2, pp. 108-117, http://dx.doi.org/10.1016/j.gfs.2014.02.001. [16]

Tschirley, D. et al. (2015), "The rise of a middle class in East and Southern Africa: Implications for food system transformation", *Journal of International Development*, Vol. 27/5, pp. 628-646, http://dx.doi.org/10.1002/jid.3107. [2]

UN DESA (2019), *World Urbanization Prospects: The 2018 Revision*, United Nations Department of Economic and Social Affairs, Population Division, New York. [11]

Worku, I. et al. (2017), "Diet transformation in Africa: The case of Ethiopia", *Agricultural Economics*, Vol. 48/S1, http://dx.doi.org/10.1111/agec.12387. [3]

4. Turning local food economies into engines for more and better jobs

Increasing demand for diversified and processed food in developing countries is an opportunity to develop the downstream sector of the agri-food industry and create quality jobs for youth. This chapter provides the rationale for the focus on local food economies and reviews some local food systems and short food supply chain business models that try to reconcile economic, social and environmental objectives. "Food co-op" business models seem to have the highest potential in terms of scalability, replicability and employment creation for developing countries.

Rapid urbanisation and a growing middle class in developing countries will increase demand for diversified, processed and nutritious food. This is an opportunity to develop the agri-food processing sector and related services that will allow local businesses to tap into this growing market. The key question is which food system model(s) offer the highest potential to create decent jobs for youth, in particular rural youth. Which model can reconcile economic, social and environmental objectives? Giving priority to youth employment creation and Sustainable Development Goals (SDGs) is a strategic choice, which can be guided by evidence on food system models that work. This chapter lays out the challenges of current food system models, including participation in agri-food global value chains (GVCs) and presents rural development initiatives and business models that can cater to local and potentially regional food demands, address social and environmental concerns and create decent jobs for youth.

Livelihoods and environmental challenges of current food systems

In most developing countries, agriculture absorbs the majority of rural workers, but low pay and poor working conditions make it difficult to sustain rural livelihoods and attract new labour market entrants. In sub-Saharan Africa, jobs in agriculture in 2019 made up for 53% of total employment, a 10 percentage point decrease from the early 2000s, while in Southeast Asia the share has nearly halved from 50% in the early 2000s to 27% in 2019 (World Bank, 2019[1]). The majority of agricultural jobs in developing countries are informal employment, with no written contract nor basic social protection. Agricultural workers are particularly more vulnerable to poor and dangerous work conditions with low and unstable incomes. Employment in agriculture is associated with the highest incidence of workers living with families below the poverty line (Altieri and Koohafkan, 2008[2]). A growing number of evidence confirms that the current food system does not produce healthy nutrition while at the same time, predominant systems of agriculture and fisheries do not provide sustainable livelihoods for many farmers and fishermen (OECD, 2021[3]; FABLE, 2019[4]; HLPE, 2016[5]).

Farming in Asia and Africa is characterised by small surfaces and low labour productivity. Out of the 570 million farms worldwide, more than 475 million farms are less than 2 hectares in size, and more than 500 million are family farms (Lowder, Skoet and Raney, 2016[6]). In Africa, small-scale farming is the norm, averaging below 3 hectares and the majority being under 2 hectares (Jayne, Chamberlin and Headey, 2014[7]). In Southeast Asia,[1] farm sizes have been declining, averaging around 3 hectares (IFAD, 2019[8]). In Viet Nam, about 85% of farms are less than 1 hectare while in Thailand farm sizes range between 1 and 5 hectares (OECD/FAO, 2017[9]). Though mechanisation is happening even in small farms, both sub-Saharan Africa and Southeast Asia lag behind in improving agricultural labour productivity (Figure 4.1). There are basically still too many agricultural workers for too little agricultural value added, resulting in lower incomes for farm households compared to other sectors (FAO, 2020[10]). As the major source of employment for most of the rural population, an increase in agricultural productivity and wages would reduce poverty rates, expand non-farm employment opportunities, and spur structural transformation and further economic development (World Bank, 2018[11]; Jayne et al., 2019[12]; Wineman et al., 2020[13]). As countries develop, employment within the food chain tends to shift from agriculture to other segments of the food chain, and jobs created outside of agriculture are often still connected to the food system (Reardon and Timmer, 2012[14]; OECD, 2021[3]). Decent job creation and SME growth in downstream segments of value chains as well as development and diversification into high-value crops will need to be key focus of policy makers (IFAD, 2019[8]; FAO, 2015[15]).

Figure 4.1. Agriculture labour productivity, by region, 2000 and 2016 (in constant 2004-05 USD)

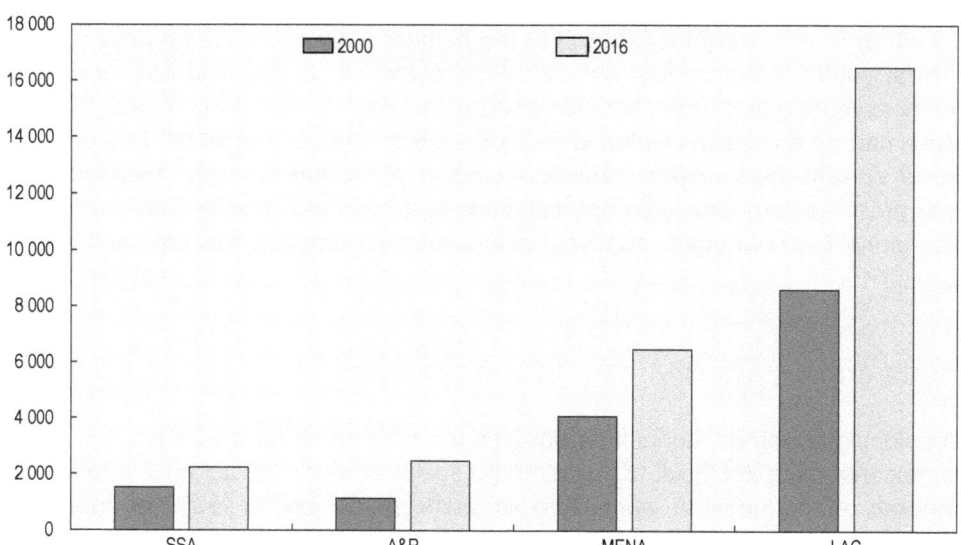

Note: SSA: Sub-Saharan Africa; A&P: Asia and the Pacific; MENA: Middle East and North Africa; LAC: Latin America and Caribbean
Source: Calculated from Agricultural total factor productivity growth indices for individual countries, 1961-2016, IFPRI (2020), *Agricultural Total Factor Productivity (TFP), 2000-2016.*

For many Asian countries, change in consumption patterns created new business opportunities in the downstream segments of the global agri-food value chain, but not necessarily for small scale farmers. Since the 1960s, the region's overall agricultural production grew twice as fast as the global average, with a consequent increase in its share of world trade in agricultural produce (de Koninck and Rousseau, 2013[16]). In Malaysia, Thailand and Viet Nam for example, agribusiness now accounts for more value added in the economy than agriculture and is a source of employment for many farm households (FAO, 2018[17]). The process of structural transformation of the food economy in Southeast Asian countries has followed similar trajectories: countries start with heavy government intervention and then liberalise to develop large processing sector focused on transformation, with an important component of FDI (Reardon, 2015[18]). For the majority of countries, policies largely consisted in various forms of support to agricultural intensification practices and territorial expansion, including maritime (de Koninck and Rousseau, 2013[16]).

In Viet Nam, economic reforms undertaken under the *Doi Moi* (renovation) from 1986 started to change centrally-planned agricultural co-operatives towards more market-reliant independent farms. A combination of policies, including land-use rights to farmers, access to credit, and openness to trade placed Viet Nam as one of the world's top rice exporter. However, participation in the export business was limited to a handful of national and provincial state-owned entreprises (OECD, 2015[19]). Private sector involvement in this export trade was encouraged only from late 2000s. The Agricultural Restructuring Plan (ARP) of 2013 started the massive investment towards a more "industrial" food system by creating more linkages between large-scale production and trade, shifting the focus away from smallholder family farms. This vertical integration of supply chain took the form of contract farming in the case of livestock, and large industrial private firms in the case of dairy, with government support for credit, training and other services (IIED and IFAD, 2016[20]). In addition, the government pioneered programmes to distinguish products based on origin (as part of food safety certification schemes) and terroir (as part of geographic indication schemes) (Delphine, 2015[21]). For the 2030 horizon, Viet Nam wants to make processed and other value-added products 50% of agri-food exports, doubling its current share (World Bank, 2016[22]).

Such rapid growth models have come with social and environmental challenges, however. The governments push for modern food distribution to promote food safety, tax revenue and competitiveness, tends to exclude small-scale producers, low-income producers and the dense network of informal traders and SMEs in between (de Koninck and Rousseau, 2013[16]; IIED and IFAD, 2016[20]). Indeed, regulations affecting the food processing segment has accelerated consolidation of the sector towards large-scale processors and resulting in the disappearance of many small fims (Reardon et al., 2014[23]). In addition, 85% of the world palm oil production comes from Southeast Asia. The rapid expansion of agriculture land has led to deforestation which has been devastating on biodiversity (UNEP, 2011[24]; Mendes-Oliveira et al., 2017[25]), while working conditions on these large plantations are often characterised by serious decent work deficits, including poor safety and health, low wages and informality (ILO, 2015[26]).

The present trajectory of growth in agricultural production is environmentally unsustainable, while the demand for food, feed, fibre and agricultural goods and services is continuously increasing. Population and income growth over the past two centuries led to large increases in food consumption and production, causing intensive and extensive use of land with negative environmental consequences such as deforestation, erosion and resource depletion (Kirch, 2005[27]; Campbell et al., 2017[28]; IPBES, 2019[29]; IPCC, 2019[30]); in (OECD, 2021[3]). Soil changes can occur naturally but are under increasing threat from a wide range pressure caused by human activities and poor soil management practices (FAO and ITPS, 2015[31]). Monoculture, intensive tillage, short to no fallow, and reduction or absence of crop rotation systems has resulted in the unsustainable degradation of soils, causing environmental harm, and decreasing the ability to respond to other environmental stresses (Kopittke et al., 2019[32]). In sub-Saharan Africa, soil degradation due to poor soil management and low use of quality fertilisers are believed to be expanding at an alarming rate and is the root causes of declining agricultural productivity in the region. The marginal increase in cereal production is due mostly to area expansion rather than yield increases (FAO and ITPS, 2015[31]).

Crop production is negatively impacted by climate change-induced rain patterns and higher frequencies of temperature anomalies, to the extent that in some cases most of the technology-generated yield gains are offset (Hoffman, Kemanian and Forest, 2018[33]). Climate change impacts the physical ability to exercise agricultural activities through the effect of rising temperature on human physiology (ILO, 2019[34]). Western Africa and Southeast Asia are projected to be among the most affected regions, as their related losses in agricultural labour productivity due to heat stress are expected to reach approximately 8.9% and 9.1% respectively by 2030. At the same time, the effect of drought on agricultural labour markets is expected to increase unrest and armed violence by approximately 4% across a sample of 58 African and Asian countries (Berman, Bonnet and Borino, n.d.[35]).

The challenge with upgrading from low value-added to high value-added participation in agri-food global value chains

Developing countries are increasingly integrated into agri-food global value chains. OECD research shows that agricultural trade is following other sectors and becoming organised within GVCs where agricultural raw material transformation and production of food for consumption occur ever more across different countries (OECD, 2020[36]). While developing countries have been progressively integrating into agri-food GVCs, for many, particularly in Africa, participation has been limited to low value upstream activities. The GVC position index measures the level of involvement of a country (or industry) in vertically fragmented production. The index is determined by the extent to which the country (or industry) is upstream or downstream in the GVCs, depending on its specialisation. A country lies upstream if it produces inputs and raw materials for others, provides manufactured intermediates or both. A country lies downstream if it uses a large share of intermediates from other countries to produce final goods for export. Figure 4.2 shows that despite a large participation in agriculture GVC (Panel A), the GVC position index records a higher positive value for the majority of African countries (Panel B), which indicates that most of them lie upstream, in low value-added activities (Balié et al., 2019[37]).

Figure 4.2. Agri-food global value chain participation index, by region, 1995, 2005 and 2013

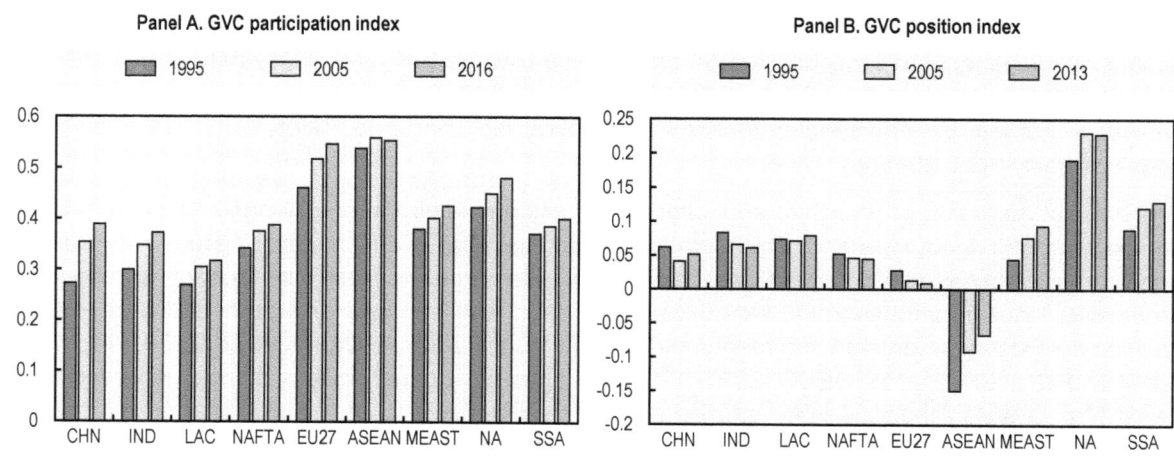

Note: The higher (or lower) the value of the GVC participation index, the larger (or smaller) is the participation of a country in global supply chains. The GVC position index is the difference between the forward and backward participation. Countries with high forward relative to backward participation record a positive value and therefore lie more upstream in the value chain.
Source: Balié et al. (2019[37]), "Does Trade Policy Impact Food and Agriculture Global Value Chain Participation of Sub-Saharan African Countries?", *American Journal of Agricultural Economics*.

At the aggregate level, trade liberalisation can be a powerful driver of economic growth and job creation (OECD, 2020[36]), but the impact on the quality of jobs and income distribution depends largely on how a country is integrated in the global value chains and for most developing countries who participate in low-skilled, low-value part of the chain, "value capture" – the share of value added in exports that remains in domestic hands – can be relatively small (AUC/OECD, 2019[38]; AfDb, OECD and UNDP, 2014[39]; OECD/WTO/UNCTAD, 2013[40]). Technological changes are making manufacturing more capital- and skill-intensive, lowering the capacity of manufacturing to absorb large amount of unskilled labour and informal workers. Global supply chains may help entry into manufacturing for low-cost countries through FDI, but they also reduce linkage with the rest of the economy and potential for the development of local upstream suppliers (Rodrik, 2014[41]).

Upgrading participation in agri-food global value chains through higher value activities proves to be extremely difficult for new entrants, particularly from developing countries. On the one hand, processing or export activities for many cash crop, such as cocoa, cotton, coffee, and sugar, require reliable cold chain and quite heavy logistic services. Value chain of these crops are tightly controlled by lead producer firms (i.e. producer-driven chains), and at present higher-value activities are predominantly performed outside of Africa (AfDb, OECD and UNDP, 2014[39]). On the other hand, entry cost in the form of initial investment needed to meet requirement for traceability and international certification, makes it difficult for many small firms to participle and thrive in export markets (AUC/OECD, 2019[38]). Firm-level data (excluding the oil sector and services) show that the top 1% accounted for 57% of country exports on average in 2014, the top 5% exceeded 80% of country export revenues on average, and the top 25% accounted for virtually all country exports (UNCTAD, 2018[42]).

Most developing countries participate in GVC in the primary production phase and the scope to increase value-added through processing/manufacturing or by acquiring new skills in research and development or marketing proves to be extremely difficult. There are two main reasons for that: First, the scope to increase value-added through processing/manufacturing depends a lot on sectors/technology. In other words, not all processing/manufacturing automatically leads to higher value added nor direct employment and there are large differences in the level of direct employment creation and value added in processing industries by sector (Figure 4.3). Sector-specific market characteristics and the type of technology that is being used can be more or less capital and skill-intensive. In Côte d'Ivoire, the scope to create direct jobs in export-oriented cocoa processing is more limited than processing of fruits or coffee. Second, the capital, skilled labour and infrastructure needed to upgrade agriculture and develop the agri-food processing sector is lacking. Looking at the successful examples of upgrading in GVCs (e.g. horticulture, organic or other certified products), securing price premiums on agricultural products therefore seems to be the most promising option and so far the one that has proven to work for developing countries.

Figure 4.3. Employment intensity of agri-food sectors in low income countries and in Côte d'Ivoire

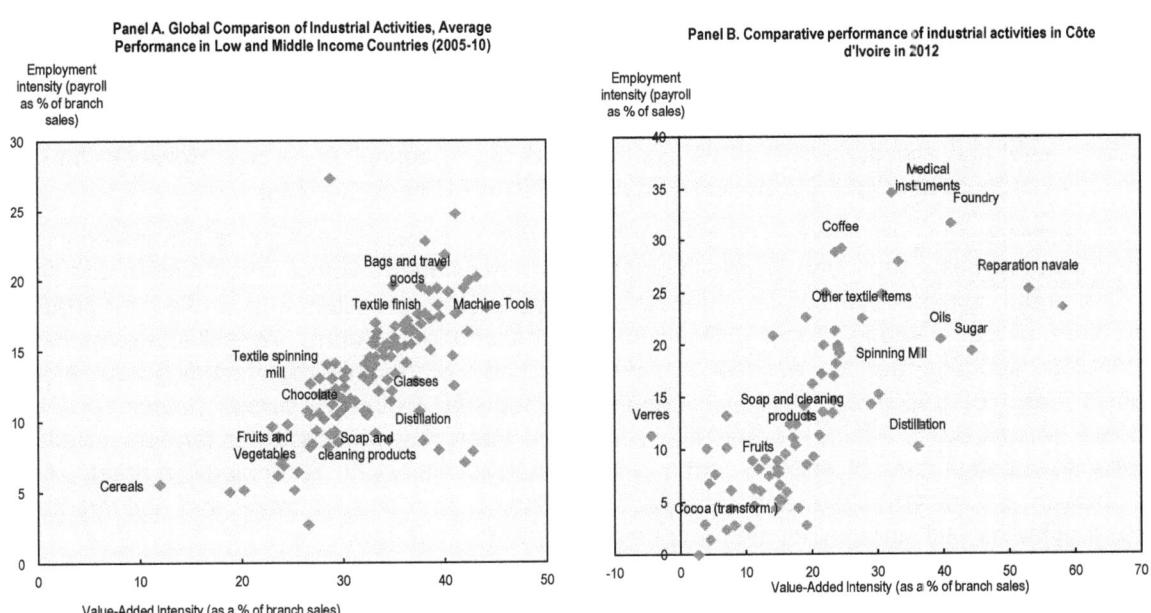

Source: OECD (2016[43]), *Multi-dimensional Country Review of Côte d'Ivoire.*

For the agri-food sector, tapping into the regional market may provide more opportunities for small and medium businesses and smallholders to participate. Plurilateral trade agreements such as the Regional Comprehensive Economic Partnership (November 2020), EU-MERCOSUR (June 2019) and the African Continental Free Trade Agreement (AfCFTA; January 2021) have been gaining momentum and driving further trade liberalisation. The AfCFTA aims at achieving a single continental market and applying zero-tariffs for 97% of all regionally traded products by 2030. This development has clear implications for the food economy, as processed food is the class of goods currently facing the highest tariffs and non-tariff barriers in the region (World Bank, 2020[44]). By 2035, the full operationalisation of the AfCFTA is expected to increase regional trade in processed food by 91% and 49% in agricultural goods, relative to a hypothetical non-agreement baseline (World Bank, 2020[44]).

Moving up agriculture in the global value chain will require structural changes but investments in agriculture and rural development are slow to come. Investments in fundamental capabilities such as skills, education, administrative capacity and governance are needed for domestic industries to emerge and structural transformation to be sustainable (Rodrik, 2014[41]). In addition to meeting humanity's basic needs for food and fuel, agriculture employs more than one in three of the world's workers, and provides livelihoods for rural households totalling 2.5 billion people (FAO, 2013[45]). Agriculture remains also an important contribution to the GDP in developing countries. In sub-Saharan Africa, the share of agriculture to the GDP was 14% in 2019 and 7.8% in developing Asia 7.8%, while in OECD countries it averaged around 1.4% (World Bank, 2019[1]). Yet, development strategies often undermine agriculture and rural development and investment in agriculture and rural infrastructure and services continues to lag behind. One of the indicators used to assess the progress made in investing in agriculture is the agricultural orientation index (AOI), which calculates the ratio of the agriculture (including forestry, fishing and hunting sector) share of government expenditure over agriculture share of GDP. Despite its importance in employment generation and food security, AOI for sub-Saharan Africa shows a gradual decline in government expenditure for agriculture, from 0.25 in 2001 and 0.18 in 2010 and to 0.14 in 2013 (AU et al., 2017[46]). AOI is less than 1 for most world's regions, indicating a lower public investment in the sector compared to its contribution to the economy, and is particularly low in sub-Saharan Africa compared to other regions (0.29 for Southeast Asia and 0.41 for developed regions) (AU et al., 2017[46]). In 2003, African Union (AU) heads of state ratified the Comprehensive Africa Agriculture Development Programme (CAADP), Africa's policy framework for transforming the agriculture sector and achieving broad-based economic growth, poverty reduction, and food and nutrition security. CAADP sets two main targets: achieving a 6% annual agricultural growth rate at the national level and allocating 10% of national budgets to the agriculture sector. However, so far, the annual investment averaged 3% between 2008 and 2016 (AU et al., 2017[46]).

Other evidence such as road density per square kilometre, access to energy, telephone connectivity, piped water or basic sanitation facilities point to under investment in basic infrastructure and services in rural areas, making it difficult for small farmers and rural communities to improve their productivity and retain or attract young people. Difficulty in securing land tenure rights, low skills development, low technology adoption, and low access to markets are some of the challenges holding back a broader transformation of rural areas in African countries (Kyomugisha, 2008[47]; Anderson, Learch and Gardner, 2016[48]; World Bank, 2018[11]; Jayne et al., 2019[12]). Improving prospects for farmers entails more profitable management of existing farms, with enhanced access to technology, markets, finance, information and infrastructure, and consolidation of land n land administration and documentation of tenure rights as well strengthening of rental markets (IFAD, 2016[49]).

The domestic and regional food market opportunity

The domestic and regional food markets in Africa offer huge opportunities for investment and job creation (World Bank, 2013[50]). In West Africa, food demand has increased five-fold since the 1960s, and the entire food economy (as defined in this report: production, processing, marketing and food-away-from-home segments) represented a total of USD 178 billion in 2010, equivalent to 36% of the regional GDP, with food import representing only 6.5% of this total domestic demand. Forty percent of the value added in the food economy was generated by non-agricultural activities (Allen and Heinrigs, 2016[51]). Despite increasing food import trends in Africa, the domestic consumption is still largely supplied by domestic and regional markets and remains a source of great growth opportunities for local businesses. Local SMEs can enjoy relative advantage owing to their proximity to, and their knowledge of the home market and local consumers' preferences. In fact, Africa's domestic and regional markets, including agri-food related business opportunities are attracting international investors beyond the continent's endowment in natural resources. The potential of domestic and regional markets attracted

53.4% of new foreign direct investment projects to Africa in 2013-17. This share is similar to Asia's level (55.7%) and ten percentage points higher than Latin America and the Caribbean's (44.8%) (AUC/OECD, 2018[52]). If the increased attention to African agriculture and agribusiness is matched with adequate electricity and irrigation as well as smart business and trade policies that link small-scale farmers with consumers in a fast urbanising Africa, the sector could contribute USD 1 trillion by 2030 to the region's economy, compared to USD 313 billion in 2010 (World Bank, 2013[50]).

The changing dynamics of the food economy in Asia and the Pacific will require the development of sustainable agri-food systems that can cater for a large urban middle class. Asia and the Pacific had achieved tremendous economic growth and poverty reduction over the past several decades. In East Asia and the Pacific, the prevalence of extreme poverty[2] declined from 61% in 1990 to 2% in 2015, while in South Asia it declined from 47% in 1990 to 16% in 2013 (World Bank, 2019[1]). The share of agriculture value added in the overall economy also declined from 14% in early 2000 to 7.8% in 2020 (World Bank, 2020[53]). Urbanisation in the region is happening more rapidly than in any other part of the world, increasing from 30% in 1990 to 47% in 2016, with further increases projected between now and 2050 (FAO, 2020[10]). By 2030, 76% of the population in Asia and the Pacific will belong to the "global middle class" (see Chapter 3). Per capita income growth comes with dietary changes whereby greater income increases the demand for nutritious and processed foods more rapidly than traditional staples (Muyanga et al., 2019[54]; Reardon et al., 2019[55]; Hernandez et al., 2018[56]; Popkin, 2017[57]). City life also leads to changes in consumption patterns and lifestyle, with urban dwellers asking for more convenient and processed foods. The share of expenditures on food prepared outside of the home has increased rapidly over the past 10 to 15 years in East and Southeast Asia, by about 15% in countries like China, Indonesia, the Philippines, Thailand and Viet Nam (FAO, 2018[17]). The private sector estimates a cumulative investment requirement of USD 800 billion between now and 2030, of which 70% for improving the quality of food, including aspects such as food safety, nutrition and sustainability and the rest for increasing quantity to feed its population. Spending on food consumption for 2030 in the region is projected at over USD 8 trillion (PWC, 2019[58]).

The COVID-19 crisis which started at the beginning of 2020 called for the need to reflect on the role of domestic and global food supply chains in order to ensure national food security. Export restriction measures taken by some food-exporting countries (e.g. Kazakhstan holding on to their flour and wheat, India and Viet Nam to their rice, and Cambodia to their fish and rice) raised concerns about the state of global food security (Dixon, Stern and Kumenov, 2020[59]; OECD, 2021[60]). The United Nations and the World Trade Organization warned that this could have devastating effects on food-importing countries. Export restrictions can alter the balance between food supply and demand, resulting in price spikes and increased price volatility. These measures are particularly damaging to low-income, food-deficit countries and to the efforts of humanitarian organisations to procure food for those in desperate need (FAO, WHO and WTO, 2020[61]). Lockdowns and movement restrictions within countries and across borders have disrupted national and local food and agricultural output and input markets further exacerbating the fragility of systems (including agri-food systems) and livelihoods (FAO, 2021[62]).

The crisis demonstrates the need to reflect on the need to strike the right balance between domestic, regional and global food supply chains in order to ensure national food security. It is especially important that international food trade not be constrained in a crisis or "weaponized by those countries that are exporters" (HLPE, 2016[5]). Countries that depend on food imports were especially vulnerable to international supply chain disruptions caused by COVID-19 (HLPE, 2016[5]). While some of these countries face real ecological limitations to producing more food at home, many have the opportunity to better balance their food sourcing portfolios (Clapp, 2017[63]). Considering the specificities of each country with respect to their capacity to produce and/or import food, it is important to provide adequate policy space for governments to pursue policies that minimise risks associated with dependence on imported food and to build greater food system resilience (HLPE, 2016[5]). As part of monitoring local food system status and prevailing practices during COVID-19 FAO conducted a global survey[3] between

April and May 2020 to map local responses. The survey finds that 38% of the responding cities indicated facilitation of direct purchases from local producers as one of the key measures to mitigate the impact (FAO, 2020[64]). One common lesson for developing countries' national agri-food sector from the COVID-19 is the pressing need to invest in efficient logistical system in transportation, storage, access to markets and handling (Nigeria, Sudan, Zimbabwe). Improving domestic storage capacity also increases countries' ability to ensure food availability through crises (Viatte et al., 2009[65]). In high income countries, the food system has proven to be resilient despite unprecedented short-term stresses put by the COVID-19 on food supply chains around the world. Nevertheless, the COVID-19 crisis has signalled the urgency to deal with the "triple challenge" of simultaneously providing food security and nutrition to a growing global population faced by the food system, ensuring the livelihoods of millions of people working along the food chain from farm to fork, and ensuring the environmental sustainability of the sector (OECD, 2021[60]).

The contribution of different local food system models in advanced economies

In many European and more advanced economies, consumers are increasingly asking for the origins of what they consume. The demand for local or regional agricultural products, both fresh and processed, are rising. The 2017 Eurobarometer survey shows that more and more Europeans are favouring regional and quality food products. More than three-quarters (77%) say respect for local tradition and "know-how" is an important factor in their decision to buy food products, 76% say having a specific label ensuring quality is important, and 75% say coming from a known geographic area is important in their decision to buy food products (Eurobarometer, 2017[66]). In 2015, the European Parliamentary Research Service found that 15% of farmers sold half of their products through these short food supply chains (European Union, 2016[67]).

The development of local food systems based on short food supply chain (SFSC) models is gaining ground in Europe. Food systems refer to "the entire range of actors and their interlinked value-adding activities involved in the production, aggregation, processing, distribution, consumption and disposal of food products that originate from agriculture, forestry or fisheries, and parts of the broader economic, societal and natural environments in which they are embedded" (FAO, 2018[68]). SFSCs are broadly understood as including a minimal number of intermediaries (or none in the case of direct sales from the producer). As SFSCs gain increasing recognition as an area to be supported within EU rural development policy, an official definition was adopted under Article 2 of Regulation (EU) No 1305/2013 on support for rural development by the European Agricultural Fund for Rural Development (EAFRD), which entered into force with the reformed Common Agricultural Policy for 2014-2020 and is defined as follows: a short supply chain means "a supply chain involving a limited number of economic operators, committed to cooperation, local economic development, and close geographical and social relations between producers, processors and consumers" (European Union, 2013[69]). In several recent resolutions, the European Parliament has expressed its support for short food supply chains and local markets as a way to ensure a fair price for producers and reconnect food products with their locality of origin (European Union, 2016[67]). An important dimension of SFSCs models is the concept of "local food", which is normally perceived as one of the pillars (UNIDO, 2020[70]).

The European Union is responding to consumer demands for more local and sustainable food supply chain models through high-level commitments and new initiatives. The European Green Deal is a set of policy initiatives by the European Union to make Europe the first climate-neutral continent by 2050. It maps a new, sustainable and inclusive growth strategy to boost the economy, improve people's health and quality of life, care for nature, and leave no one behind. The Farm to Fork Strategy is one of the key components of the Green Deal, together with the EU Biodiversity Strategy for 2030. The Farm to Fork strategy recognises the intrinsic links between healthy people, healthy societies and a healthy planet and calls for a shift to a sustainable food system to bring environmental, health and social benefits, as well as economic gains and to ensure that the recovery from the crisis is on a sustainable path. The strategy points to the importance of sustainable livelihoods for primary producers, who still lag behind in terms of income, as an essential factor for successful recovery and transition (EU, 2020[71]). It aims at slashing pesticide use by 50% and increase organic farming by 25% by 2030. The Green Deal calls for 40% of the Common Agricultural Policy (CAP) budget to be dedicated to climate actions. The Farm to Fork strategy foresees the development of a legislative framework for a sustainable food system for 2023. The EU programmes like LEADER (Liaison Entre Actions pour le Développement de l'Economie Rurale), a key pillar of the European Agricultural Fund for Rural Development, started in the early 1990s, continue to support rural development projects using local development method whereby local actors are involved in the design and implementation of strategies, decision making and resource allocation for the development of local areas (European Union, 2016[67]).

The budget for SFSC is gradually increasing within the Common Agricultural Policy budget. CAP accounts for one third of the EU's total budget and is the largest subsidies schemes the EU runs. CAP consists of two main pillars, the first one dedicated to direct hectare-based payments to farmers and the second one to rural development, under which SFSC and organic agriculture initiatives fall. The EU budget for 2020 was a total of EUR 168.68 billion in commitment appropriations, with the CAP accounting for 34.5% (EUR 58.12 billion). Direct payments to farmers accounted for 70% of the total CAP budget (EUR 40.6 billion) and rural development measures for 25% (EUR 14.6 billion) (EU, 2021[72]). The CAP reform for 2021-27 foresees a decrease in the total CAP budget by 15% compared to 2014-20, i.e. an 11% cut for direct payments and a 28% cut for rural development. The proposed changes would nonetheless allocate 75% of the total CAP budget (EUR 324.2 billion) to direct payments and 21% to rural development (EU, 2021[72]). In the next CAP budget (2023-27), EUR 340 million will be allocated for conversion of conventional agriculture to organic agriculture (Agence Bio, 2021[73]).

Local food systems can take several forms: farmers' markets, vegetable box schemes, community-supported agriculture, food co-operatives (or supermarkets that source primarily locally), online retail platforms as well as public procurement schemes which source food locally. They can be regrouped into four broad categories according to the lead actor: producer-led, government-led, consumer-led and retailer-led (Figure 4.4). All of these have the territorial embeddedness and short food supply chain as a common denominator, meaning they aim to reinforce the capacity of agri-food systems to bring value to specific territorial resources and re-kindle social relations of proximity (Watts et al., 2005[74]) in (Lamine, 2015[75]). This section describes some of the common business models sprouting in many advanced economies that favour local production, processing and distribution. Not all models manage to reconcile economic, social and environmental objectives, however, as the middle class grows in developing countries, these are interesting to study as alternative business models that could be more inclusive of smallholder producers and local small and medium entreprises.

Figure 4.4. Local agri-food business models

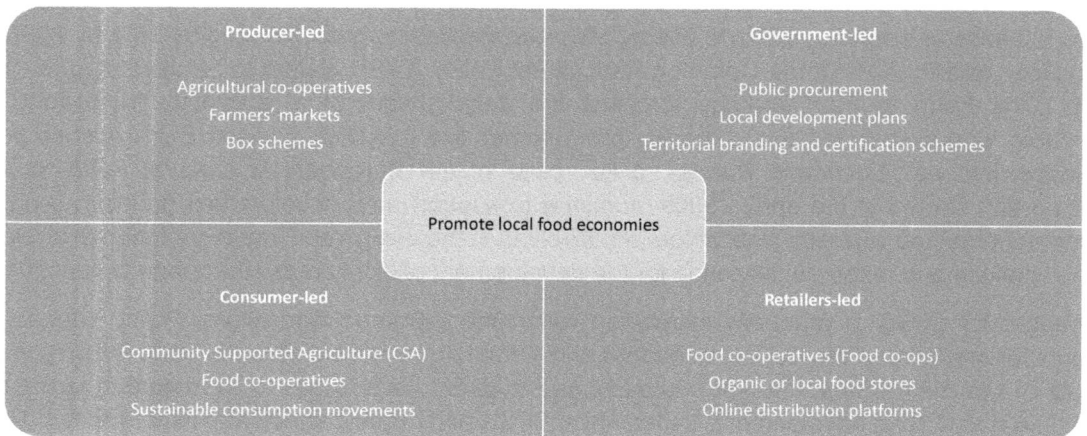

Note: List non-exhaustive.
Source: Authors' elaboration.

Producer-led models

Agricultural co-operatives or farmers' organisations are important institutions for the livelihoods of small scale farmers and to ensure sustainable food economies. A co-operative is an autonomous association of persons united voluntarily to meet their common economic, social and cultural needs and aspirations through a jointly owned and democratically controlled enterprise (ILO recommendation 193, 2014[76]). Co-operatives can be formed by a group of producers, customers, employees, users or residents. Members share equal voting rights regardless of the amount of capital they put into the enterprise. Co-operatives are businesses driven by values and not just profit, as such they put fairness, equality and social justice at the heart of the enterprise (ICA, 2014[77]). Co-operatives offer support to their members in the form of training, information, access to market and credits and natural resources. They also help build soft skills such as making decisions, negotiating prices and contracts, and understanding land rights (FAO, 2012[78]). More than nine out of ten farms in the world are family farms, representing the dominant form of farming in most countries (FAO, 2014[79]). In developing countries, co-operatives play a particularly important role for small scale farmers and marginalised groups of people such as youth and women by providing sustainable employment and improving their livelihoods. According to Agriterra, an organisation that supports the development of co-operatives in developing countries, between 2016 and 2019, the share of women employed in co-operatives increased from 29% to 33% and the share of youth employed increased from 48% to 55% (Table 4.1).

Table 4.1. Evolution of female and youth employees within co-operatives in selected developing countries

N	Year	Permanent staff	Female staff	% Female	Youth staff	% Youth
185	2016	5 086	1 491	29%	2 440	48%
220	2017	7 259	2 317	32%	3 525	49%
277	2018	7 786	2 275	29%	3 776	48%
278	2019	6 978	2 295	33%	3 822	55%

Note: N refers to the number of farmers' organisations registered with Agriterra (50% from Africa, 30% from Asia and 20% from Latin America.
Source: Agriterra (2021), Interview with Agriterra.

Co-operatives also play an important role in facilitating job creation and rural development. The value of co-operatives beyond an economic role is widely acknowledged (Levin, 2003[80]). Co-operatives exist in various forms ranging from small-scale to multi-million-dollar businesses across the globe. Globally, the International Co-operative Alliance (ICA) counts over 3 million co-operatives that provide quality employment to over 280 million people (ICA, 2020[81]; ICA World Cooperative Report, 2020[82]). Agriculture co-operatives can also be multi-purpose.

For example, the National Agricultural Co-operative Federation, known as *Nonghyup* (NH) in Korea, is the world's third largest agricultural co-operative (ICA, 2014[77]). What started as a government-led initiative after the Korean war to overcome chronic food shortages, is now a multi-purpose service provider that promotes rural development through banking, insurance, agricultural marketing and extension services. As of April 2017, NH counted 2.25 million members from 1 131 primary agricultural co-operatives, representing more than 80% of Korean farmers (OECD, 2013[83]). NH is largely credited for the modernisation of agriculture and rural communities. The agricultural marketing service which includes direct distribution outlets called Hanaro Mart is the co-operative's most successful line of business and benefits its members. The direct sales outlets help keep lower prices for consumers while ensuring fair prices to farmers (ICA, 2014[77]). Profits from the primary agricultural co-operatives are accrued to the banking and insurance business, while profits from financial business in turn support input supply and marketing business of primary co-operatives (KREI, 2015[84]). In view of its objective to provide mutual support among small-scale farmers, primary co-operatives have been exempted from certain provisions of the Monopoly Regulation and Fair Trade Act. For example, joint purchase and sale activities by co-operatives are subject to tax reduction or exemption in the following: value-added tax applied to agricultural inputs and equipment; sales tax; interest income and dividend income on deposits and contributions of members; and corporate income tax (OECD, 2018[85]).

Agricultural co-operatives strengthen bargaining power, voice and representation of producers. In developing countries, agriculture co-operatives were promoted widely in the 1990s with mixed results. Co-operative organisations were for a large majority promoted by governments without genuine participation from members. As a result, the members were often alienated from what should have been their own organisations, with little or no influence on issues such as the marketing and pricing of their products (FAO, 1998[86]). The heavy involvement of governments was considered harmful and many countries revised their policies concerning co-operatives on the principles of participation, and consultancy rather than intervention (FAO, 1998[86]). Co-operatives, when operated by their members and self-financed, are proving to be effective and today their numbers keep growing both as producers' organisations but also financial service providers. Agricultural co-operatives strengthen bargaining power, voice and representation of producers. For example, the role of coffee co-operatives has been critical in negotiating fairtrade agreements with developed countries and raising the price of Ethiopian coffee (Dahlberg, 2011[87]). In remote areas where farmers have limited access to markets, farmers organised as co-operatives can have stronger bargaining power against private traders.

Consumer-led models

Community Supported Agriculture (CSA) is a system that connects farmers directly with the consumers in a partnership that shares the risk of production. Consumers subscribe to a yearly harvest before planting season and receive a portion of whatever is available each week of the growing season. As such, consumers accept to share the risks associated with agricultural production as well as the benefits from over-abundance. CSA was coined in the United States (US) but is also known as *AMAP* (Association pour le maintien d'une agriculture paysanne) in France, *teikei* (meaning 'co-operation') in Japan, and *food guilds* in Switzerland. It is an alternative model of food production and distribution, which is often linked to organic farming and short circuit distribution. CSA started in 1985 with 2 farms and grew to 1 900 in 2008 (Local Harvest, 2008[88]) and 6 200 in 2014 (Local Harvest, 2014[89]). CSA still represents less than 1% of farms in the United States. CSAs are usually initiated by consumers by creating an association and recruiting a core group of 'clients', who will then look for the producer(s).

An impact study of CSA on farmers revealed mixed outcomes (Brown and Miller, 2008[90]). The 2001 national survey of CSA found that 96% of the CSA farms used organic methods, almost 75% of the farmers had a college degree, and CSA farmers were more likely to be female or younger (on average ten years younger) than US farmers. Sixty three percent of CSA farms had gross farm income greater than USD 20 000. Nevertheless, only about 46% of the surveyed farmers were satisfied with their ability to cover operating costs. Almost half (48%) were unsatisfied with their own compensation from the farm. A majority of respondents (57 %) were satisfied with their quality of life and said that their CSA operation improved this quality. A 2018 study, which evaluated the livelihoods of CSA farmers from the farmers' perspective in the Connecticut River Valley of Massachusetts, found similar results. CSA farmers earned far below the median national income and generally fail to earn a living wage. CSA farmers, however, valued the broader social, ecological, and economic benefits to farming as a source of well-being (Paul, 2019[91]).

Most CSA farmers have to diversify their sources of income. Studies show inadequate farmer earnings and support from the members in the community (Lass et al., 2003[92]; Tegtmeier and Duffy, 2005[93]; Jarosz, 2008[94]; Feagan and Henderson, 2009[95]). CSA provides operational cash flow but is the lowest source of income (Flora and Bregendahl, 2012[96]). A survey of CSAs in California showed that farmers use an average of 3.3 market outlets: CSA, farmers' markets, on-site sales, mail order/Internet, other direct-to-consumer sales, direct-to-retail sales, wholesale market sales, and services and other non-farm-good sales (Galt, 2016[97]). In France, an evaluation of AMAPs also showed similar results in terms of profitability. While they provide a steady source of income and a saving on direct marketing costs, the annual contractual agreement between producers and consumers on quality, quantity and diversity represents a pressure on profitability. In fact, the profitability of an AMAP is highly dependent on the way the transaction (or risk) costs are divided between producers and members in the contract (Olivier and Coquart, 2010[98]).

CSAs' profitability is not independent of the local market. Indeed, competition from conventional supermarkets as well as other Alternative Food Networks (AFN) negatively affects CSAs. With the increase in the number of local and organic outlets in both mainstream and alternative grocery retailers, consumers have more choices and price points will eventually fall as per the rule of competition if nothing is done to take into account social and environmental externalities in the price. A survey of 111 CSAs in California found that certain AFNs undermine some of CSA's fundamental values, such as fair farmer compensation and strong member-farmer relationships (Galt, 2016[97]), reducing the profit of producers.

From an environmental perspective, CSAs have had clearly a positive impact on farmers and their lands. As the model calls for it, CSA farmers depend on multiple crops both to cater for their membership and as a risk-hedging strategy. According to the 2018 study, CSA farmers grew an average of 38 crops and 115 varieties (Paul, 2019[91]). Farmers claimed that crop diversification is a way of assuring some profit along with environmental benefits. Farmers assured that biodiversity improved the quality of the soil, reduced pest infestations, allowing for a reduction of inputs, improved water retention and sustained healthy soil (Paul, 2019[91]).

From a societal perspective, the link between producers and consumers lies at the heart of this model. CSAs have been strengthening social cohesion particularly in rural and remote areas but also in cities where consumers are increasingly asking to know more about the source of their products. One of the key social benefits perceived by consumers is the link between food and health. Fresh and seasonal food is considered to have dietary benefits as it is more nutritious than food preserved for a long time (FAAN, 2010[99]), though, depending on the commodity, poorly conserved fresh food may have less nutritional value than canned food (Rickman et al., 2007[100]). Organic farms, which are usually the CSA model, tend to be more labour intensive therefore generating more employment per hectare. In France, the organic food industry has had progressive growth during the past decade. Between 2014 and 2019, organic farms have more than doubled in surface from 1.1 million hectares to 2.3 million hectares, creating more than 30 000 full time jobs, while employment in the conventional agriculture has continuously been in decline. The number of total direct jobs in the organic food sector, including production, processing, retail and services was estimated at 179 503 in 2019, a 14% increase year-on-year since 2016 (Agence Bio, 2021[73]).

Awareness raising around sustainable consumption and production have also helped bring value back to territorial specialties and the "made in local" culture, as well as change dietary habits. The movement "Slow Food", started in Italy by active citizens, spread across countries and has now become a global trade mark symbolising ecological consumption. The Slow Food movement started in Italy in the 1980s with the intention to protect local food traditions and cultures, counteract the rise of fast life and combat people's dwindling interest in the food they eat. The movement has since had a global impact with millions of people joining from over 160 countries. Slow Food believes food is tied to many other aspects of life, including culture, politics, agriculture and the environment. The movement contributes to the sustainable consumption and production debate and to the preservation of regional and local varieties, foods and lifestyles. Several studies (Debs, 2013[101]; Hall, 2012[102]; Dumitru et al., 2016[103]) evaluated the impact of Slow Food on consumption patterns, the environment and society, and find that the movement has contributed in raising the profile of a number of issues, particularly the significance of local food and fair trade purchasing for restaurants and hotels as well as consumers in general. Changing food demand is more difficult than changing food supply, however change in diet is possible through a combination of tools for behavioural change and actions across whole food systems (Vermeulen et al., 2020[104]).

The major benefit from the process of localising food systems is the re-balancing of power and knowledge relationships in food supply systems that have become distorted or abstract by the increasing distance and lack of social and physical connections between producers and consumers (Dumitru et al., 2016[103]). Valorising local food systems provides an important impetus to reflect on where society is going and where new opportunities for consumption and production lie (Van Der Meulen, 2008[105]). The Slow Food movement has also had a positive influence on a new wave of young people who have become 'food producers' as farmers themselves or food self-provisioning. These new young farmers innovate with agriculture techniques and use online sale-systems and create "food communities" (Dumitru et al., 2016[103]). Farmers who have joined the movement particularly appreciate the knowledge the network provides in preserving the biodiversity of their cultivated and wild varieties and using local resources at the farm and reducing chemical inputs that may damage the quality of their products. Farmers in the Middle Eastern and Latin American farmers observed improvements in income and managerial skills as the most relevant impact, while African farmers underlined mainly the use of local resources (Debs, 2013[101]).

Retailer-led models

Food co-operatives, better known as "food co-ops" are a rising trend in co-operative food systems. A food system can be understood as an interdependent group of activities that include the production, processing, distribution, wholesaling, retailing, consumption, and disposal of food. A co-operative food system connects these activities through a common value of working together for mutual benefits based on democratically chosen goals (Sumner, 2014[106]). Though several forms of collaboration and business models exist within the co-operative food systems, food co-operatives hold a central place. Food co-ops are retail grocers that operate on very specific values and motivations. Because they are not owned by shareholders, the economic and social benefits of their activity stay in the communities where they are established. Profits generated are either reinvested in the enterprise or returned to the members (ICA, 2021[107])(ICA website). They are typically owned by consumers who are members of the co-operatives. Food co-ops operate with members who volunteer a fixed number of hours per month (usually three hours per month), thereby decreasing fixed costs of the business. Decisions are made by all members who have equal voting rights. In the US, between 2008 and 2018, 134 new co-ops opened with a 74% success rate, representing 160 000 new member-owners within the community-owned grocery stores nationwide, and 100 more were expected in 2019 (Steinman, 2020[108]). Park Slope Food Coop, is perhaps the best known pioneer of this model, having started in Brooklyn, New York in 1973 and still thriving with 17 000 stores today. In Europe co-operative grocery stores are steadily sprouting (Kauffman, 2017[109]; Potet, 2018[110]; Briquet, 2020[111]). Though they currently take up a small percentage of the market, their growth is sustained year-on-year. In France, *La Louve*, the first consumer-led co-operative started in France in 2016, counts today 5 000 active members and increased its revenues from EUR 3.9 million in 2017 to EUR 7.2 million in 2019 (Nippert, 2020[112]). In Norway and Sweden, co-operative supermarkets already comprise 20-30% of the grocery retail market (Voinea, 2015[113]).

Food co-ops stimulate local economic development. One common characteristic of food co-ops is their anchorage on the "local" and they cater for a highly localised consumer base. This is a conscious choice coherent with the values of democracy, environmental integrity and community resilience (Sumner, 2011[114]). They usually adhere to the Rochdale principles such as voluntary membership, democratic governance, limited return on equity and concern for the community. A study on 350 food co-ops in the United States concludes that food co-ops are important business organisations that contribute to the intensification of local food networks and producer-consumer relations (Katchova and Woods, 2013[115]). Food co-ops also help democratise the organic and local food markets by giving access to quality food to a wider range of consumers.

Food co-ops tend to pay higher wages to their employees. A study carried out by ICA in 2012 based on 165 co-operative food stores in the United States, combined with industry market research showed that the average food co-op creates 9.3 jobs for every million dollars in sales, compared to a conventional grocer, which creates only 5.8 jobs per million dollars in sales. Conventional grocers tend to rely more on automation and centralised management functions including human resources, accounting, and purchasing. The study found that co-op stores generally paid comparable or slightly higher wages to their employees compared to conventional grocers. Considering the average wages of all employees including bonuses and profit sharing, co-op employees earned an average of about USD 1.00 per hour more than their peers in the conventional sector (COOP, 2012[116]).

Multi-stakeholder food co-operatives can provide the necessary infrastructure to bring local producers, processors and consumers to construct a co-operative food system. Co-operative networks such as Biocoop in France and Ontario Natural Food Co-op in Canada have diverse stakeholders who are co-op members (Sumner, 2014[106]). A network can have producers, processors, shop owner and consumers as equal stakeholders. Such structures have been able to bring these different actors along the value chain at the negotiating table to discuss the "fair price" of food. These retailers are taking increasingly more share of the food distribution market (see Box 4.1).

Box 4.1. Inclusive food retail distribution model: Biocoop, France

In 2018, 7.5% of the agricultural area of the EU was grown organically (Agence Bio, 2019[117]). In France, today, the organic food industry still represents only 6.5% of the food retail distribution but it is a fast growing sector. The French organic market was estimated at EUR 13 billion in 2020, and despite COVID-19, it was 10.4% increase from 2019. Between 2012 and 2020, organic food consumption by households increased close to five times. The sector also employs about 200 000 people (a 1.6 fold increase from 2016) both on and off-farm. More than half (128 000) of these jobs are on-farm, while the rest are jobs in the downstream sector of the distribution (26 000 in processing; 43 200 in distribution;

and 2 300 in services such as consulting, research and development and training). Organic food products sales have increased on average by 16% year-on-year since 2015 (Agence Bio, 2021[73]).

Biocoop is the largest organic food retail distributor, but stands out from the conventional supermarkets in its governance structure. Biocoop started in the early 1980s as a consumer co-operative in two regions in France. In 1984, this consumer-led initiative turns into 40 stores and in 1986 Biocoop changes its status to association, becoming the first organic food distributor in France. In 2002, Biocoop had over 200 stores and its legal status changed to public co-operative entreprise (société anonyme co-operative).

The governance structure of Biocoop is unique and incorporates a diverse group of stakeholders. Four types of Biocoop members co-exist: store owners (419), salaried associates (433), associations of consumers (3) and producer groups (20). Each of the 875 members has one vote. Store owners are independent entrepreneurs and do not pay royalties to Biocoop like in a franchise model. The producer groups bring together 3 200 farms in four value chains (fruits and vegetables, meat, milk and cereals) and participate in all decision making and in the development of Biocoop's strategic plans.

Despite diverging interests, members work together towards the common objective of developing organic agriculture by 1) increasing the supply of organic local food products; 2) practising fair pricing to facilitate organic food consumption; 3) sharing profits through the co-operative model; and 4) reducing negative impacts of their activities on the environment.

Figure 4.5. Bioocoop revenues and employment

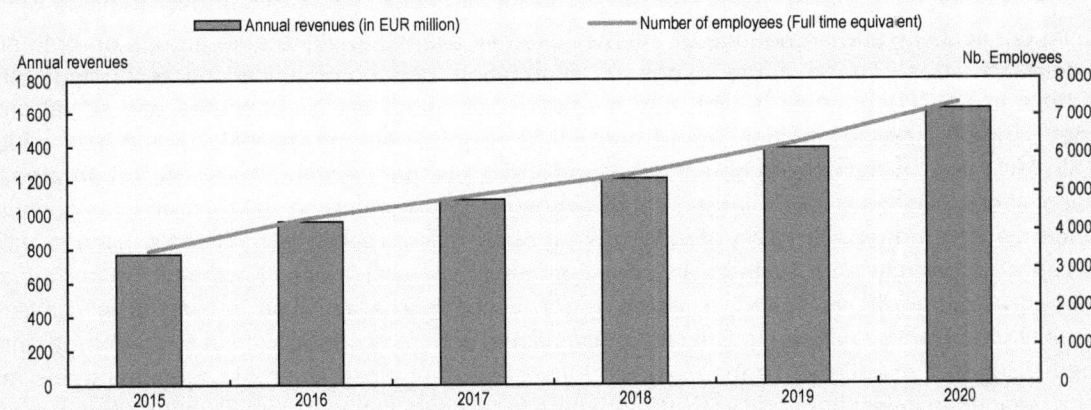

Source: Interview with Pierrick De Ronne, President of Biocoop, 2021.

In 2020, Biocoop had an annual revenue of EUR 1 600 million. The number of employees has increased in proportion to its growth. In 2020, Biocoop had 678 stores, which generated a total of 7 332 full-time equivalent jobs. The headquarters employs 1 162 persons.

Eighty percent of the products sold in Biocoop stores are from France with 15% of the products from within 150 km distance. Twenty percent of all products have the fairtrade label. Each store is obligated to respect the Biocoop Charter and store compliance requirements.

Biocoop's long term vision is to change the current food system structure into one that works for farmers, food processors and distributors, and consumers and to ensure that all people along the agri-food value chain are able to have decent livelihoods. The Biocoop business model promotes the come back of organic farming as the mainstream of agriculture, while respecting the social contract and the environment and revitalising local economies and small enterprises through inclusive procurement policies.

Source: Biocoop (2019[118]); *Rapport d'Activité et Déclaration de Performance Extra-Financière 2019* ; Interview with Pierrick De Ronne, President of Biocoop, in 2021.

E-distribution platforms have seen a huge boost in recent years and use of their services peaked particularly during the COVID-19 crisis. Food distribution is increasingly impacted by e-commerce (Rickman et al., 2007[100]). Food and grocery products are among the top ten items purchased online, with clothing, footwear and sporting goods have experienced fast growth in recent years (OECD, 2017[119]). E-distribution platforms can contribute to local economic development particularly if the business model supports local producers and local entrepreneurs. Moreover, the COVID-19 pandemic has increased the demand for local products. In France, e-distribution platforms like La Ruche Qui Dit Oui or smaller regional initiative like Loco Motivés, have seen the number of members increase by 150% (L'info durable, 2020[120]). La Ruche Qui Dit Oui launched the first short food supply platform in France in 2011. The products travel on average 49 km, and 30% of them are organic. The producer gets 80% of the sale tag, the "hive" manager 8.35% and the platform 11.65% and this seems to work for everyone, including consumers. The ten year-old platform counts over 200 000 regular users and works with over 5 000 local producers who supply 850 distribution points called 'hives'. Other smaller regional initiatives promoting short food supply chain models have been more successful using online shopping options than the traditional box schemes (see CSA above and Box 4.2. on Loco Motivés).

Unequal connectivity and knowledge of Internet use risk alienating vulnerable groups on both supply and demand sides. The average usage of information and communications technology among individuals in OECD countries is high but unequally distributed across countries and social groups. Internet usage for online purchases and banking is very low among the elderly and less educated (OECD, 2017[119]). In developing countries, where the digital gap between rural and urban areas and between social classes is even larger, rapid exposure to e-commerce risks creating unsustainable dependence and further alienation of vulnerable groups. The experience of China's Taobao Villages shows the opportunity and vulnerability of e-commerce in rural areas. E-commerce in China has developed at extraordinary speed in recent years. E-commerce activities in rural areas have been intensively promoted by Alibaba (a Chinese multinational company specialised in e-commerce) through Taobao Villages. Essentially, Taobao are rural villages, often close to urban agglomerations, where Alibaba decided to invest hard and soft infrastructure to facilitate the commercialisation of local products via the internet. The number of Taobao Villages rose exponentially from 20 in 2013 to 1331 in 2016. The initial success of some Taobao Villages in helping local agricultural producers, handicraft entreprises and family businesses deserves attention. New job opportunities have also been created in the service sector related to e-commerce such as graphic design, photography, delivery, storage and information technology (IT) technicians. However, several studies raise concerns on the economic sustainability of Taobao Villages, pointing to the homogenisation of products, cut-throat competition amongst producers and lack of innovation (Zeng et al., 2015[121]; Li and Zhang, 2015[122]). There is also rising concern that the increasing dependence of rural e-tailers on Alibaba's infrastructure will put them in a disadvantaged position vis-à-vis the multinational IT conglomerate in the long-run, as well as undermine the culture of local communities (Li, 2017[123]).

> **Box 4.2. Linking local producers with consumers through the digital platform: Loco-Motivés in France**
>
> Created in 2012 to provide direct links between producers and consumers in the region of Aveyron, Loco-Motivés created a website with eight producers and a dozen clients. Only one year later, the association deliveried on average 50 baskets of orders per week. In 2020, Loco-Motivés connected directly about 40 producers with more than 2 500 consumers, while continuing its short food supply chain model. Each week, the association delivers on average 250 to 280 baskets of orders, consisting of fresh produce (fruits, vegetables and meat) and processed meat, cheese, jam, wine, syrup, oil, honey, etc. Their sales shot up five times during COVID-19 confinements.
>
> Loco-Motivés is a membership-based association with 200 members and an administrative council which consists of 28 associate producers and four volunteer consumers. The objective of the association is to promote direct sales of local agricultural products. Participating producers are small-scale producers and 80% of the products offered are organic or certified "Nature and Progress". The association currently employs three full-time employees who handle logistics, the deliveries and the management of the Internet platform. The clients are not obliged to buy each week as is the case in a CSA/AMAP, and can select the products they want to order.
>
> Loco-Motivés received a start-up support grant of EUR 16 000 from the Fondation de France and EUR 6 000 from the Community of Communes (communauté de communes) to buy the delivery trucks. A Community of Communes is a public institution that regroups several French communes to promote inter-communal co-operation. Other than these seed funds, Loco-Motivés is financially self-sustainable. It receives membership fees but mostly functions through the commission from sales. The association takes a commission of 15% to 30% on the sale price, with the commission fee varying depending on whether the producer is a member of the association. The price is determined by the producer.
>
> Since its start in 2012, Loco-Motivés's revenues from local products have skyrocketed from EUR 13 000 the first year to EUR 460 000 in 2019. This new sales outlet has allowed some of the producers to diversify their production and earn additional revenues. Member producers, depending on the type of production, can make between 5% and 50% of their total revenues from Loco-Motivés platform. The customers, instead of driving up to 30 minutes to the nearest market, can get their orders delivered at a place closer to their homes.
>
> The regular exchange among producers has been a rich source of knowledge in terms of production methods and has motivated farmers to adopt more sustainable and ecological farming practices. Some producers are in the process of converting their farms into organic agriculture. The cohesion among producers is at the core of Loco-Motivés' success. However, with a growth rate of 25% per year, the logistics are complex, with storage space becoming inadequate for the volume handled and the need for additional full time staff becoming more pressing. The challenge for Loco-Motivés will be to keep its core values of cohesion while growing bigger.
>
> Source: Interview with Stéphanie Degoute, founder of Loco-Motivés, in 2021.

Government-led models

Public procurement can be a strategic tool to support sustainable local economic development. Public procurement refers to a range of contractual arrangements and purchasing tools used by governments to plan, source and manage the acquisition of goods, services and works. It represents an average of 12% of GDP in OECD countries and 20-30% in developing economies (OECD, 2020[124]). About 63%

of public procurement occurs at the sub-national level, with almost 134 000 authorities at local and regional level across the OECD (OECD, 2019[125]). Public procurement is increasingly used to promote responsible business conduct and address global supply chain risks to people and the planet. "Green" and "sustainable" public procurement refer to the introduction of environmental and social considerations in making public procurement decisions. Specifically, green public procurement is the purchase of "products and services which are less environmentally damaging when taking into account their whole life cycle" (OECD, 2015[126]), while sustainable public procurement also looks at employment opportunities, working conditions and social inclusion (EC, 2011[127]).

Ensuring social and environmental considerations into public procurement drives local and regional food economies. The European Union Directive 2014/24/EU on public procurement makes provisions to consider other criteria that 'price', such as quality, social, environmental and innovative aspects as well as delivery conditions and process (EU, 2014[128]). National laws may add other binding rules for public procurement. Various initiatives can be found in the EU countries to support local and regional food economies. The study "Sustainable public procurement of food" reviews the food procurement system for public schools in ten countries (Soldi, 2018[129]). The following are some of the more striking examples. The procurement process in Rome, Italy, for the provision of food and catering services to public school canteens is valued at over EUR 374 million for the period 2017-20. Since 2001, Rome has gradually turned to organic food for its school food procurement system, allocating 49 points out of 100 to qualitative criteria other than price. In Slovenia, the region of Podravje has set the target of increasing the consumption of locally grown food in public school canteens to 20% by 2020 and to 70% by 2030. In Lens, France, the quality-price ratio in the procurement requirements of food for school canteens was 70:30, with the minimum requirement for organic food set at 20%. Other innovative approaches by municipalities exist, which go beyond school canteens to support small scale farmers (see Box 4.3 on Brazil).

Box 4.3. Sourcing local to support food aid programmes in Brazil

Since 2003, Brazil has implements a food procurement programme called Programa de Aquisiçao de Alimentos (PAA). PAA purchases food from small-scale and vulnerable farmers for food aid programmes. PAA gives priority to the most vulnerable producers, farmers' organisations run by women and indigenous populations. The programme works with various government ministries, as well as provincial and municipal governments, civil society organisations, co-operatives and workers' unions.

The programme is managed by a committee composed of the Ministry of Agriculture, Livestock and Food Supply; the Agrarian Development Agency; the Ministry of Social Development and Fight against Hunger; the Ministry of Economy; and the Ministry of Planning, Budget and Management.

The procurement process is done through two schemes:

1. The Direct Purchase scheme contributes to building the food reserves of the federal government. These stocks are used to meet the government's own needs, such as for the distribution of food baskets to victims or vulnerable social groups like landless families and indigenous people.
2. The Purchase for Simultaneous Delivery scheme is for any project that does not require storage and the purchased products can be delivered immediately to the targeted beneficiaries. The contracted small scale farmer therefore delivers the products directly to food insecure populations, nurseries, public hospitals, schools, etc.

Given the success of PAA, in 2009, the government also introduced national school feeding legislation. Brazil's National School Feeding Programme (PNAE) aims to purchase at least 30% of the food for school meals from local small-scale farmers. Key success factors of PNAE are its inclusive policy, which facilitates farmers' participation, and the strong co-ordination between ministries of education, agrarian development, social development, agriculture and health. The eligibility to be a contractor for either of these programmes (PAA or PANAE) requires obtaining the Declaration of Aptitude to the National Program for Strengthening Family Agriculture (Declaraçao de Aptidão or DAP). The DAP is a certificate which attests that the producer is a family farm or an association of family farms, according to criteria set by the Family Units of Agrarian Production (UFPA).

Source: Swensson (2015[130]), "Institutional Procurement of Food from Smallholder Farmers: The Case of Brazil".

Territorial branding and certification schemes have attracted increasing attention from policy makers, trade negotiators and agricultural producers. Roquefort, Darjeeling, Cognac, Champagne are some well-known names associated throughout the world with products of a certain nature and quality, known for their geographical origin and for having characteristics linked to these territories. Geographical Indication (GI) or Protected Designation of Origin (PDO) is a form of intellectual property given to a product that has a specific geographical origin and possesses qualities or a reputation that are due to that origin. GI protection is granted through the Trade Related Aspects of Intellectual Property Rights (TRIPS) Agreement. In order to function as a GI, a sign must identify a product as originating in a given place. In addition, the qualities, characteristics or reputation of the product should be essentially due to the place of origin. Since the qualities depend on the geographical place of production, there is a clear link between the product and its original place of production. A GI enables those who have the right to use the indication to prevent its use by a third party whose product does not conform to the applicable standards. This form of intellectual property (IP) now appeals to more and more nations as a tool to upgrade in GVCs, including African and Asian countries, but essentially for export markets. A key challenge will be the capacity of developing countries to invent and manage new institutions that could enforce the rules, controls and sanctions of GI, with a clear distribution of roles between private, collective and public stakeholders (Sautier, Biénabe and Cerdan, 2011[131]). GI recognition is also dependent of existing trade agreements making it a complex and difficult process for producer organisations in developing countries to obtain.

Other less costly territorial branding methods exist that could cater to domestic markets. Producers can differentiate themselves by marketing the "local' or "organic" nature of their products. "Genussregionen" (Austria), "Distinctly Cumbrian" (England), "Living Tisza" (Hungary) are examples of non-statutory territorial branding that can make quality branding more accessible to small farmers with limited resources (FAAN, 2010[99]). Products standards such as regional labels, organic labels or controlled designation of origin allow the recognition of a particular product coming from a specific geographic area, and could potentially support value addition and the development of local value chains in developing countries.

Territorial branding contribute to rural development. Regional producers become entitled to use a territorial brand (GI or other forms) and the added value generated accrues among all such producers. Because officially recognised brands usually generate a premium price, they contribute to local employment creation, which ultimately may help to prevent rural exodus. In addition, branded products also have important spin-off effects, for example in tourism, creating additional jobs. Territorial brands may bring value to a region not only in terms of jobs and higher income, but also by promoting the region as a whole, contributing to the creation of a "regional brand" (WIPO, 2017[132]). Kampot pepper, produced in the Kampot province in Cambodia, won GI status in 2010. Since gaining GI status, prices for Kampot pepper increased from USD 5 per kilogramme before GI status in 2010 to about USD 18 per kilogramme in 2014, helping livelihoods of small farmers (OECD, 2018[133]).

Conclusion

The different models presented above represent a small sample of many local food economy and business models found in advanced economies in Europe and the United States. Not all succeed in addressing producers' livelihoods, environment, social cohesion and job creation objectives equally, but they all have more or less positive effects on one or several of these aspects. Agricultural co-operatives, food co-operatives, public procurement models and territorial branding and certification schemes have a strong consideration to improve producers' livelihoods. CSAs tend to value more environmental impact and social cohesion and often remains small-scale due to the very nature of the business model which is based on a direct annual contract between the producers and consumers. E-distribution platforms have allowed to create more direct linkages while overcoming the physical distance and contractual obligations, but at the risk of some suppliers in remote areas becoming dependent on the platform.

Creation of new quality wage jobs is not well-evidenced in many of these model. Based on existing data, food co-operatives (both consumer- and producer-led) seem to be the most promising in terms of scalability and job creation. Environmental footprint seems to also be an important consideration in this model, as these 'food co-ops' operate with charters requiring a certain quantity of local, organic, and low-carbon products, though no independent evaluation can attest to this yet. Territorial branding and certification schemes require strong involvement of local governments and "champions", and as such, need careful co-ordination between the different actors in the value chain. Certification schemes like GIs have the highest potential for direct and indirect job creation through new local business development for domestic and export markets as well as tourism.

Development strategies need to strike a balance between developing effective local food systems that will allow local business opportunities to tap into the growing domestic demand and pursuing export-oriented growth based on commodities. Upgrading in GVCs through premium products (GI certified or organic) has seen some successes in developing countries, but in the majority of cases, participation in GVCs in low-value agricultural commodities has little spillover-effects on domestic value added and jobs. The changing domestic consumption patterns and rising incomes in many developing countries have turned attention to the inclusive development potential of local value chains to tap into domestic and regional markets. In advanced economies, there is an increasing consumption trend for organic, local and low-carbon footprint foods, and though still representing a minority share, the year-on-year demand increase has seen various local business and territorial development initiatives sprout. The chapter reviewed the most common ones with replicability potential in developing countries.

Many of the local food system initiatives (CSA, co-operatives, farmers' markets, and more recently e-platforms) presented in this chapter also exist in developing countries and often constitute a large part of how food is purchased and consumed in rural areas, albeit informally organised. Formalising, scaling-up, creating decent incomes and jobs through existing models have faced obstacles. In more advanced countries, scaling-up and creating quality wage jobs while keeping short supply chains and local values at the core of the business model have been possible through a combination of government-supported regulations and rising producers and consumers' consciousness and desire for sustainable local alternatives. Success factors of "food co-op" distribution models and e-platforms, for example, lie primarily in having built strong cohesion between producers and consumers through shared values. Other factors such as rural infrastructure, advanced logistical and transport services, and digital connectivity are necessary to create an enabling environment.

Building a sustainable local food system means more investment in local production and transformation, diversification of agriculture products and upgrading skills of young people in rural areas in downstream segments of agri-food value chain. All this needs to be accompanied by an overarching development strategy that prioritises agriculture, local food systems, rural development and youth employment. This is a political choice that needs to be made by individual countries.

Notes

[1] Indonesia, Viet Nam, Thailand, The Philippines, Myanmar and Lao PDR.

[2] Defined as people living on less than USD 1.90 [2011 purchasing power parity] per day

[3] The survey obtained 860 responses from a wide range of city sizes across countries at different income levels (16% low-income countries, 41% lower middle-income countries, 32% upper middle-income countries and 11% high-income countries) and geographical locations (Latin America and the Caribbean, Africa, Asia and the Pacific, Europe and Central Asia, and the Near East and North Africa).

References

AfDb, OECD and UNDP (2014), *African Economic Outlook 2014: Global Value Chains and Africa's Industrialisation*, African Development Bank; Organisation for Economic Co-operation and Development; United Nations Development Programme, Paris. [39]

Agence Bio (2021), *Les chiffres 2020 du secteur bio*. [73]

Agence Bio (2019), *Organic Farming and Market in the European Union*. [117]

Allen, T. and P. Heinrigs (2016), *Emerging Opportunities in the West African Food Economy*, Organisation for Economic Co-operation and Development, Paris. [51]

Altieri, M. and P. Koohafkan (2008), *Enduring Farms: Climate Change, Smallholders and Traditional Farming Communities*, Third World Network, Penang. [2]

Anderson, J., C. Learch and S. Gardner (2016), *National Survey and Segmentation of Smallholder Households in Uganda: Understanding Their Demand for Financial, Agricultural, and Digital Solutions*. [48]

AUC/OECD (2019), *Africa's Development Dynamics 2019: Achieving Productive Transformation*, OECD Publishing, Paris/African Union Commission, Addis Ababa, https://dx.doi.org/10.1787/c1cd7de0-en. [38]

AUC/OECD (2018), *Africa's Development Dynamics 2018 : Growth, jobs and inequalities*, OECD Publishing. [52]

AU et al. (2017), *2017 Africa Sustainable Development Report: Tracking Progress on Agenda 2063 and the Sustainable Development Goals,*, African Union; Economic Commission for Africa; African Development Bank; United Nations Development Programme, Addis Ababa. [46]

Balié, J. et al. (2019), "Does Trade Policy Impact Food and Agriculture Global Value Chain Participation of Sub-Saharan African Countries?", *American Journal of Agricultural Economics*, Vol. 101/3, pp. 773-789, https://onlinelibrary.wiley.com/doi/10.1093/ajae/aay091. [37]

Berman, N., A. Bonnet and F. Borino (n.d.), "Climate, agricultural labour makets and conflict (forthcoming)", *ILO Working Paper*, ILO, Geneva. [35]

Biocoop (2019), *Rapport d'Activité et Déclaration de Performance Extra-Financière 2019*, https://www.biocoop.fr/Biocoop/Rapport-d-activite-et-de-developpement-durable2. [118]

Briquet (2020), *Les coopératives sont en pleine croissance!*, Sudinfo. [111]

Brown and Miller (2008), *The impacts of local markets: A review of research on farmers markets and community supported agriculture (CSA)*, http://dx.doi.org/10.1111/j.1467-8276.2008.01220.x. [90]

Campbell, B. et al. (2017), "Agriculture production as a major driver of the Earth system exceeding planetary boundaries", *Ecology and Society*, Vol. 22/4, http://dx.doi.org/10.5751/ES-09595-220408. [28]

Clapp (2017), "Food self-sufficiency: Making sense of it, and when it makes sense", *Food Policy*, Vol. 66, http://dx.doi.org/10.1016/j.foodpol.2016.12.001. [63]

COOP (2012), *Healthy Foods Healthy Communities Measuring the Social and Economic Impact of Food Co-ops*, http://www.strongertogether.coop. [116]

Dahlberg (2011), *Ethiopian Coffee and Fair Trade-An empirical study*. [87]

de Koninck, R. and J. Rousseau (2013), "Southeast Asian Agricultures: Why such Rapid Growth?", *Espace géographique*, Vol. 42/2, http://dx.doi.org/10.3917/eg.422.0143. [16]

Debs (2013), *Analysis of the Slow Food movement impact on the farmers and rural areas' sustainable development Presentata da: Philipp Debs*. [101]

Delphine, M. (2015), *Linking farmers to market with geographical indications and trademarks in Vietnam.*. [21]

Dixon, R., D. Stern and A. Kumenov (2020), "As borders harden during pandemic some countries look to hold onto their own food", *The Washington Post*. [59]

Dumitru et al. (2016), *WP 4 | CASE STUDY Report: SLOW FOOD MOVEMENT*. [103]

EC (2011), "Buying Social A Guide to Taking Account of Social Considerations in Public Procurement", http://dx.doi.org/10.2767/18977. [127]

EU (2021), *Fact Sheets on the European Union*. [72]

EU (2020), *Farm to Fork Strategy*, European Union. [71]

EU (2014), *DIRECTIVE 2014/24/EU OF THE EUROPEAN PARLIAMENT AND OF THE COUNCIL of 26 February 2014 on public procurement and repealing Directive 2004/18/EC (Text with EEA relevance)*. [128]

Eurobarometer (2017), "Special Eurobarometer 473 Special Eurobarometer 473-Wave EB88.4-TNS opinion & social Europeans, Agriculture and the CAP Report Fieldwork", http://dx.doi.org/10.2762/68892. [66]

European Union (2016), *Short food supply chains and local food systems in the EU*. [67]

European Union (2013), "Regulation (EU) No 1305/2013 of the European Parliament and of the Council of 17 December 2013 on support for rural development by the European Agricultural Fund for Rural Development (EAFRD) and repealing Council Regulation (EC) No 1698/2005", *Official Journal of the European Union*. [69]

FAAN (2010), *Local Food Systems in Europe: Case studies from five countries and what they imply for policy and practice*, Interdisziplinäres Forschungszentrum für Technik (IFZ), Graz. [99]

FABLE (2019), *Pathways to Sustainable Land-Use and Food Systems*, International Institute for Applied Systems Analysis (IIASA) and Sustainable Development Solutions Network (SDSN), Luxemburg and Paris. [4]

FAO (2021), *COVID-19 Country profiles*, https://www.fao.org/2019-ncov/resources/country-profiles/en/?page=3&ipp=5&tx_dynalist_pi1%5Bpar%5D=YToxOntzOjE6IkwiO3M6MToiMiI7fQ%3D%3D (accessed on 10 November 2021). [62]

FAO (2020), *Cities and local governments at the forefront in building inclusive and resilient food systems*, http://dx.doi.org/10.4060/cb0407en. [64]

FAO (2020), *State of Food and Agriculture in Asia and the Pacific Region, including Future Prospects and Emerging Issues. Thirty-fifth Session of the FAO Regional Conference for Asia and the Pacific*, Food and Agriculture Organization of the United Nations, Bhutan. [10]

FAO (2018), *Dynamic development, shifting demographics, changing diets*, Food and Agriculture Organization, Bangkok. [17]

FAO (2018), *Sustainable food systems: Concept and framework*. [68]

FAO (2015), "Agricultural transformation of middle-income Asian economies: Diversification, farm size and mechanization", *ESA Working Paper*, No. 15-04, Food and Agriculture Organization, Rome. [15]

FAO (2014), *The State of Food Insecurity in the World: Strengthening the enabling environment for food security and nutrition*. [79]

FAO (2013), *Statistical Yearbook of the Food And Agricultural Organization for the United Nations*. [45]

FAO (2012), *Agricultural Cooperatives: Key to Feeding the World*. [78]

FAO (1998), *Agricultural Cooperative Development - A Manual for Trainers*, Food and Agriculture Organization of the UN, Rome. [86]

FAO and ITPS (2015), *Status of the World's Soil Resources*, Food and Agriculture Organization and Intergovernmental Technical Panel on Soils, Rome. [31]

FAO, WHO and WTO (2020), *Mitigating impacts of COVID-19 on food trade and markets: Joint statement*. [61]

Feagan and Henderson (2009), "Devon Acres CSA: Local struggles in a global food system", *Agriculture and Human Values*, Vol. 26/3, pp. 203-217, http://dx.doi.org/10.1007/s10460-008-9154-9. [95]

Flora and Bregendahl (2012), *Collaborative Community-Supported Agriculture: Balancing Community Capitals for Producers and Consumers Community Based Water Management View project Center for Rural Studies View project*, https://www.researchgate.net/publication/303168822. [96]

Galt (2016), "Eroding the Community in Community Supported Agriculture (CSA): Competition's Effects in Alternative Food Networks in California", *Sociologia Ruralis*, Vol. 56/4, http://dx.doi.org/10.1111/soru.12102. [97]

Hall, C. (2012), "The Contradictions and Paradoxes of Slow Food: Environmental Change, Sustainability and the Conservation of Taste", in *Slow Tourism*, Multilingual Matters, http://dx.doi.org/10.21832/9781845412821-007. [102]

Hernandez et al. (2018), "The "quiet revolution" in the aquaculture value chain in Bangladesh", *Aquaculture*, Vol. 493, http://dx.doi.org/10.1016/j.aquaculture.2017.06.006. [56]

HLPE (2016), *Sustainable agricultural development for food security and nutrition: what roles for livestock?*, High Level Panel of Experts on Food Security and Nutrition of the Committee on World Food Security, Rome. [5]

Hoffman, A., A. Kemanian and C. Forest (2018), "Analysis of climate signals in the crop yield record of sub-Saharan Africa", *Global Change Biology*, Vol. 24/1, http://dx.doi.org/10.1111/gcb.13901. [33]

ICA (2021), *ICA website*. [107]

ICA (2020), *International Cooperative Alliance factsheets*. [81]

ICA (2014), *Exploring the Co-Operative Economy*, http://www.monitor.coop. [77]

ICA World Cooperative Report (2020), *Exploring the Cooperative Economy, Report 2020*, http://www.monitor.coop. [82]

IFAD (2019), *An Outlook on Asia's Agricultural and Rural Transformation: Prospects and options for making it an inclusive and sustainable one*, International Fund for Agricultural Development, Rome. [8]

IFAD (2016), *Rural Development Report 2016: Fostering inclusive rural transformation*, International Fund for Agricultural Development, Rome. [49]

IIED and IFAD (2016), *Food consumption, urbanisation and rural transformations in Southeast Asia*, IIED. [20]

ILO (2019), *Working on a warmer planet: The impact of heat stress on labour productivity and decent work*, International Labour Office, Geneva. [34]

ILO (2015), *Decent Work on Plantations*, International Labour Office, Geneva. [26]

ILO recommendation 193 (2014), *Promoting cooperatives : an information guide to ILO Recommendation No. 193*, ILO. [76]

IPBES (2019), *Summary for policy makers of the global assessment report on biodiversity and ecosystem services of the Intergovernmental Science-Policy Platform on Biodiversity and Ecosystem Services*, http://www.ipbes.net. [29]

IPCC (2019), *Climate Change and Land - An IPCC Special Report on climate change, desertification, land degradation, sustainable land management, food security, and greenhouse gas fluxes in terrestrial ecosystems*. [30]

Jarosz (2008), "The city in the country: Growing alternative food networks in Metropolitan areas", *Journal of Rural Studies*, Vol. 24/3, http://dx.doi.org/10.1016/j.jrurstud.2007.10.002. [94]

Jayne, T., J. Chamberlin and D. Headey (2014), "Land pressures, the evolution of farming systems, and development strategies in Africa: A synthesis", *Food Policy*, Vol. 48. [7]

Jayne, T. et al. (2019), "Are medium-scale farms driving agricultural transformation in sub-Saharan Africa?", *Agricultural Economics*, Vol. 50, pp. 75-95, http://dx.doi.org/10.1111/agec.12535. [12]

Katchova and Woods (2013), "Local Foods and Food Cooperatives: Ethics, Economics and Competition Issues", http://dx.doi.org/10.1007/978-94-007-6274-9_12. [115]

Kauffman (2017), *The rise of the modern food cooperative*. [109]

Kirch, P. (2005), "Archaeology and Global Change: The Holocene Record", *Annual Review of Environment and Resources*, Vol. 30/1, pp. 409-440. [27]

Kopittke, P. et al. (2019), "Soil and the intensification of agriculture for global food security", *Environment International*, Vol. 132, http://dx.doi.org/10.1016/j.envint.2019.105078. [32]

KREI (2015), *Agriculture in Korea*, Korea Rural Economic Institute, Naju. [84]

Kyomugisha, E. (2008), *Land tenure and agricultural productivity in Uganda*, USSP Brief, International Food Policy Research Institute, https://www.ifpri.org/publication/land-tenure-and-agricultural-productivity-uganda (accessed on 2 May 2021). [47]

Lamine (2015), "Sustainability and resilience in agrifood systems: Reconnecting agriculture, food and the environment", *Sociologia Ruralis*, Vol. 55/1, pp. 41-61, http://dx.doi.org/10.1111/soru.12061. [75]

Lass et al. (2003), *Community Supported Agriculture Entering the 21 st Century: Results from the 2001 National Survey*. [92]

Levin, M. (2003), "ILO Recommendation no. 193 on the promotion of cooperatives", *Revue Internationale de l'Economie Sociale*. [80]

Li, A. (2017), "E-commerce and Taobao Villages A Promise for China's Rural Development?", *China Perspectives*. [123]

L'info durable (2020), *De la fourche à l'assiette, le vaste réseau de circuit court de "La Ruche qui dit Oui!"*. [120]

Li, Y. and Y. Zhang (2015), "Analysis of the Role of Local Government in the Development in the 'Taobao' Village", *Science and Technology Management Research*. [122]

Local Harvest (2014), *Local harvest, real food, real farmers, real community*. [89]

Local Harvest (2008), *Local harvest, real food, real farmers, real community*. [88]

Lowder, S., J. Skoet and T. Raney (2016), *The Number, Size, and Distribution of Farms, Smallholder Farms, and Family Farms Worldwide*, Food and Agriculture Organization, Rome. [6]

Mendes-Oliveira, A. et al. (2017), "Oil palm monoculture induces drastic erosion of an Amazonian forest mammal fauna", *PLOS ONE*, Vol. 12/11, http://dx.doi.org/10.1371/journal.pone.0187650. [25]

Muyanga et al. (2019), *Feed the Future Innovation Lab for Food Security Policy Policy Research Brief on Synthesis Report III Rural and Agrifood Systems in Transforming Economies in Africa and Asia*. [54]

Nippert, A. (2020), "Quatre ans après son lancement, le supermarché coopératif La Louve attire toujours de nouveaux membres", *Le Monde*. [112]

OECD (2021), *COVID-19 and food systems: Short- and long-term impacts*, Organisation for Economic Co-operation and Development, Paris. [60]

OECD (2021), *Making Better Policies for Food Systems*, OECD Publishing, Paris, https://dx.doi.org/10.1787/ddfba4de-en. [3]

OECD (2020), *Global value chains in agriculture and food: A synthesis of OECD analysis*, Organisation for Economic Co-operation and Development, Paris. [36]

OECD (2020), *Integrating Responsible Business Conduct in Public Procurement*, OECD Publishing, Paris, https://dx.doi.org/10.1787/02682b01-en. [124]

OECD (2019), *Government at a Glance 2019*, OECD Publishing, Paris, https://dx.doi.org/10.1787/8ccf5c38-en. [125]

OECD (2018), *Innovation, Agricultural Productivity and Sustainability in Korea*, OECD Food and Agricultural Reviews, OECD Publishing, Paris, https://dx.doi.org/10.1787/9789264307773-en. [85]

OECD (2018), *The Future of Rural Youth in Developing Countries: Tapping the Potential of Local Value Chains*, OECD Publishing, Paris, https://dx.doi.org/10.1787/9789264298521-en. [133]

OECD (2017), *OECD Digital Economy Outlook 2017*, OECD Publishing, Paris, https://dx.doi.org/10.1787/9789264276284-en. [119]

OECD (2016), *Multi-dimensional Review of Côte d'Ivoire: Volume 3. From Analysis to Action*, OECD Development Pathways, OECD Publishing, Paris, https://dx.doi.org/10.1787/9789264258501-en. [43]

OECD (2015), *Agricultural Policies in Viet Nam*, Organisation for Economic Co-operation and Development, Paris. [19]

OECD (2015), *Going Green: Best Practices for Sustainable Procurement*. [126]

OECD (2013), *OECD Food and Agricultural Review: Innovation, Agricultural Productivity and Sustainability in Korea*, Organisation for Economic Co-operation and Development, Paris. [83]

OECD/FAO (2017), *OECD/FAO Agricultural Outlook 2017-2026*, OECD Publishing, Paris/FAO, Rome, https://doi.org/10.1787/1112c23b-en. [9]

OECD/WTO/UNCTAD (2013), *Implications of Global Value Chains for Trade, Investment, Development and Jobs: An OECD, WTO, UNCTAD joint report*, Prepared for the G-20 Leaders Summit Saint Petersburg (Russian Federation), Saint Petersburg. [40]

Olivier, V. and D. Coquart (2010), "Les AMAP : une alternative socio-économique pour des petits producteurs locaux ?", *Économie rurale* 318-319, http://dx.doi.org/10.4000/economierurale.2793. [98]

Paul (2019), "Community-supported agriculture in the United States: Social, ecological, and economic benefits to farming", *Journal of Agrarian Change*, Vol. 19/1, http://dx.doi.org/10.1111/joac.12280. [91]

Popkin (2017), "Relationship between shifts in food system dynamics and acceleration of the global nutrition transition", *Nutrition Reviews*, Vol. 75/2, http://dx.doi.org/10.1093/nutrit/nuw064. [57]

Potet (2018), "Des dizaines de supermarchés autogérés en projet dans des villes moyennes", *Le Monde*. [110]

PWC (2019), "The Asia Food Challenge Harvesting the Future". [58]

Reardon et al. (2019), "Rapid transformation of food systems in developing regions: Highlighting the role of agricultural research & innovations", *Agricultural Systems*, Vol. 172, http://dx.doi.org/10.1016/j.agsy.2018.01.022. [55]

Reardon, T. (2015), "The hidden middle: the quiet revolution in the midstream of agrifood value chains in developing countries", *Oxford Review of Economic Policy*, Vol. 31/1, http://dx.doi.org/10.1093/oxrep/grv011. [18]

Reardon, T. and C. Timmer (2012), "The Economics of the Food System Revolution", *Annual Review of Resource Economics*, Vol. 4/1, pp. 225-264, http://dx.doi.org/10.1146/annurev.resource.050708.144147. [14]

Reardon, T. et al. (2014), "Urbanization, Diet Change, and Transformation of Food Supply Chains in Asia", Michigan State University. [23]

Rickman et al. (2007), "Nutritional comparison of fresh, frozen and canned fruits and vegetables. Part 1. Vitamins C and B and phenolic compounds", *Journal of the Science of Food and Agriculture*, Vol. 87/6, http://dx.doi.org/10.1002/jsfa.2825. [100]

Rodrik, D. (2014), "The Past, Present, and Future of Economic Growth", *Challenge*, Vol. 57/3, http://dx.doi.org/10.2753/0577-5132570301. [41]

Sautier, D., E. Biénabe and C. Cerdan (2011), "Geographical indications in developing countries", CIRAD. [131]

Soldi (2018), *Sustainable public procurement of food*, EU. [129]

Steinman (2020), *Grocery Story: How Food Co-Ops Transformed an Industry*. [108]

Sumner (2014), "Leveraging the Local: Cooperative Food Systems and the Local Organic Food Co-ops Network in Ontario, Canada", *Journal of Agriculture, Food Systems, and Community Development*, http://dx.doi.org/10.5304/jafscd.2014.043.004. [106]

Sumner (2011), "Serving Social Justice: The Role of the Commons in Sustainable Food Systems", *Studies in Social Justice*, Vol. 5/1, http://dx.doi.org/10.26522/ssj.v5i1.992. [114]

Swensson, L. (2015), *Institutional Procurement of Food from Smallholder Farmers: The Case of Brazil*, Food and Agriculture Organization, https://www.researchgate.net/publication/325904817_Institutional_Procurement_of_food_from_smallholder_farmers_The_Case_of_Brazil. [130]

Tegtmeier and Duffy (2005), *Community Supported Agriculture (CSA) in the Midwest United States: A regional characterization Part of the Agriculture Commons, and the International and Community Nutrition Commons*, http://lib.dr.iastate.edu/leopold_pubspapers. [93]

UNCTAD (2018), *Trade and Development Report 2018: Power, Platforms and the Free Trade Delusion*, United Nations Conference on Trade and Development, Geneva. [42]

UNEP (2011), *Oil palm plantations: threats and opportunities for tropical ecosystems*, United Nations Environment Programme. [24]

UNIDO (2020), *Short Food Supply Chains for Promoting Local Food on Local Markets*, United Nations Industrial Development Organization. [70]

Van Der Meulen (2008), *The Emergence of Slow Food*. [105]

Vermeulen, S. et al. (2020), "Changing diets and the transformation of the global food system", *Annals of the New York Academy of Sciences*, Vol. 1478/1, http://dx.doi.org/10.1111/nyas.14446. [104]

Viatte et al. (2009), *Responding to the food crisis: synthesis of medium-term measures proposed in inter-agency assessments*. [65]

Voinea (2015), *Case studies: retail co-ops in Europe*, Coop News. [113]

Watts et al. (2005), "Making reconnections in agro-food geography: alternative systems of food provision", *Progress in Human Geography*, Vol. 29/1, http://dx.doi.org/10.1191/0309132505ph526oa. [74]

Wineman, A. et al. (2020), "The changing face of agriculture in Tanzania: Indicators of transformation", *Development Policy Review*, Vol. 38/6, pp. 685-709, http://dx.doi.org/10.1111/dpr.12491. [13]

WIPO (2017), *World Intellectual Property Report 2017 : Intangible Capital in Global Value Chains.*, World Intellectual Property Organization. [132]

World Bank (2020), *World Development Indicators*, The World Bank Group. [53]

World Bank (2020), *World development report 2020 : trading for development in the age of global value chains*. [44]

World Bank (2019), *World Development Indicators*, The World Bank Group. [1]

World Bank (2018), *Closing the Potential-Performance Divide in Ugandan Agriculture*, World Bank, Washington, DC, http://www.worldbank.org (accessed on 2 May 2021). [11]

World Bank (2016), *Vietnam Development Report 2016. Transforming Vietnamese Agriculture: Gaining More from Less*, The World Bank Group, Hanoi. [22]

World Bank (2013), *Growing Africa Unlocking the Potential of Agribusiness*. [50]

Zeng, Y. et al. (2015), "Study on the formation of Taobao village: taking 860 Dongfeng village and Junpu village as examples", *Economic geography*. [121]

5. Policy options to stimulate local food economies

The previous chapters showed that, in the countries examined, the majority of youth work in the food economy, mostly in agriculture, but that the highest employment growth potential is in the downstream segments of the food economy. For the local food economies to respond to the rising domestic and regional food demand and create quality jobs for youth, strengthening local food systems must become more central in national development strategies. A number of economic, social and environmental bottlenecks will need to be addressed. Policy directions are laid out to stimulate and strengthen local food economies.

The food economy represents an important source of employment for youth and particularly rural youth in developing countries, and will remain so for some time to come, especially in sub-Saharan Africa. Yet, by and large, youth jobs in the food economy remain of poor quality. The study shows that, in the countries examined, the majority of youth work in the food economy and although most of them are found in the agriculture segment, a non-negligible share are working in downstream segments in upper middle-income countries. Indeed, job forecast in the food economy for 11 sub-Saharan African countries for 2030 shows the highest employment growth in the downstream segments, but these segments start from a small base. Downstream activities also tend to attract more educated youth and women, which means that the agri-food sector could partially fulfill youth aspirations to work outside of agriculture. How can the local food economy therefore become more vibrant to respond to the rising domestic demand for diversified and nutritious food and create more quality jobs for youth both on and off farm? This calls for a number of policy actions to create a conducive environment that will boost domestic food markets to become more vibrant, productive and efficient.

Foremost, local food systems must become more central in national development strategies. Many developing countries rely on agriculture for an important share of their GDP and total employment. However, at present, only few export-led growth strategies aimed at increasing participation in agri-food GVCs have been successful in terms of spillovers to the local economies and decent job creation. Most often, value-chain specific challenges such as reliable cold chain and logistics services, access to quality inputs, and the initial investment needed to meet requirement for traceability and international certification make it difficult for many small farmers and firms in developing countries to participle and thrive in processing and higher-value activities. Given these difficulties in upgrading in the GVC and in light of the rising domestic food demand in developing countries, the local food system represents a real opportunity to tap into to meet economic, social and environmental objectives. For this, governments must first put local food systems and agri-food industries as priority investment sectors in their national development plans.

Making local food economies more vibrant so that they create a real market demand for producers and all actors along the agri-food value chain will require addressing the bottlenecks in different segments of the food economy. Interventions aimed at improving a specific segment of the value chain will not lead to long-term impact if the dysfunctionalities of the local food markets are not dealt with in a holistic manner. A systems approach that involves all actors in the agri-food value chain needs to be adopted when designing policies and programmes aimed at job creation in food economies. The policy directions listed in this section are organised by key economic, social and environmental bottlenecks that need to be tackled in order to unleash the food economy in developing countries and contribute to SDG goals 2, 8 and 12.[1]

Overcoming economic barriers

Agriculture is the largest employer of youth in many developing countries, especially in Africa, yet, youth are not wanting to farm like their parents and are turning their backs on agriculture. The biggest reason is the low earnings. Farming is associated with poverty and in order for young people to be attracted to agriculture, farming has to pay better incomes and wages. Agriculture must become an attractive business. Low farm productivity in developing countries is often cited as the main bottleneck to better earning, together with poor market linkages. Indeed, when there is a demand for local food products (raw or processed) buyers often complain of low quantity and inconsistent quality. An enabling environment for local producers and SMEs in agri-food to better access local markets is perhaps the first knot to untie. This includes facilitating better access to a range of financial products including soft loans for youth entrepreneurs to help business development, improving productivity through mechanisation and transfer of technologies and improving regulatory frameworks on food safety standards. In France, the network of Technology Resource Centres (CRT, Centre de Ressources

Technologiques) and Technology Diffusion Centres (CDT, Cellules de Diffusion Technologique) are well-established institutions which have been providing such comprehensive services for over 30 years. CRT/CDTs support small and medium entreprises to address their needs through technology transfer and equipment. However they also provide business development services such as marketing, project management, hygiene certification, link to financial services, etc. The model operates on a nominal user fee basis, with co-funding by the local governments.

Adapting the CRT/CDT model in developing countries is showing promising results. Tech-Dev, a non-profit association, provides technological solutions to micro and small and medium entreprises (MSMEs) working in food transformation in selected Sahel countries using the CRT/CDT operational model. Tech-Dev considers first and foremost the local conditions and existing actors in the entire local agri-food ecosystem in order to help MSMEs boost their business. Common assistance provided include not only the transfer of suitable technology but also support for equipment and packaging purchases, obtaining food safety checks and general business development such as access to financing and markets. A pilot project in Mali was expanded, with funding from the French Development Agency (AFD), to Burkina Faso, Sénégal and Tchad. Tech-Dev has now established seven "technology hubs" (HUB-IIT – Intégrer l'Information Technologique) which works in partnership with local institutions in these four Sahel countries. These hubs follow closely the development of 950 MSMEs in the food economy – more than 80% owned by women – and support over 1 500 MSMEs, which employ around 6 000 workers. While the core objective of HUB-IITs is the transfer of technologies to improve agri-food processing and distribution, the lessons-learned from projects led by Tech-Dev in developing countries is that the technology support must come after careful consideration of the entire agri-food ecosystem in which the business operates. Understanding the interactions between stakeholders in the agri-food value chain, the adequacy between the technology and the staff that will be using it, and the physical accessibility of the business activity are all critical elements to consider in order to ensure sustainability of the HUB-IITs support.

Improving rural-urban linkages has proven to have important spillover-effects on local economies. Taking into account the inherent interdependence of rural and urban areas can help unlock some of the bottlenecks limiting the potential of food systems. This entails strengthening linkages between rural and urban areas both through hard and soft infrastructure – including facilitating access to urban services (for rural dwellers), improving market linkages between the two territories and facilitating the flows of goods and services as well as circular mobility between rural and urban areas. Intermediary cities (as well as small towns) play a critical role in this process as they are located close to rural areas, and are often linked to their rural hinterlands through formal and informal supply chains (OECD, 2016[1]); (OECD/PSI, 2020[2]). Intermediary cities (or small and medium size cities) play a critical role in food economies as they facilitate access to markets for rural producers, and are often the nodes that connect rural areas to urban services and to national and international markets. Intermediary cities also serve as entry points to agricultural supply chains for small holder farmers and also play important roles in creating off-farm employment for rural and urban dwellers (OECD, forthcoming[3]).

Countries like Ethiopia, Rwanda and South Africa have recognised the potential of intermediary cities and developed explicit strategies targeting the development of intermediary cities (Government of Rwanda and GGGI, 2015[4]; COGTA, 2016[5]; OECD/PSI, 2020[2]). Ethiopia is one of the least urbanised countries in sub-Saharan Africa, but thanks to intermediary cities Ethiopia is urbanising at an unprecedented rate. The Government of Ethiopia has put deliberate efforts to boost intermediary cities through national development and urban plans since the early 2000s as well as spatial plans to develop seven intermediary cities with high potential to function as poles for economic and urban growth (OECD/PSI, 2020[2]). Moreover, in 2015, the Government launched the Integrated Agro-Industrial Parks programme, with the plan to develop agro-processing parks in small and medium size cities. The programme aimed at boosting the commercialisation of the agricultural sector, increasing rural job creation and reducing rural poverty while also building agricultural value chains (UNIDO, 2015[6]).

Overcoming social barriers

The majority of jobs in the food economy are of poor quality. In developing countries, informality is pretty much the norm for youth working in the food economy, and it is particularly high in the agriculture segment. As youth move to jobs in the downstream segments, the pay scale improves, the skills gap narrows and informality decreases. Notwithstanding the importance of improving jobs in agriculture, more investment in the processing, marketing and food-away-from home segments of the food economy will likely create jobs that better match youth career aspirations. In sub-Saharan Africa, the share of students studying agriculture is equal to that of OECD countries at 2%, while agriculture contributes 14% to Africa's GDP compared to 1.4% in Europe (AfDB et al., 2012[7]). Youth skills development to improve labour matching along the agri-food value chain will need to become about holistic food system education that goes beyond agricultural techniques or production yields, but teaches complex issues of ecological sustainability, food safety and security, food sovereignty, and emerging changes to food systems including production and distribution using digital technology (HLPE, 2020[8]). Food system education programmes are being implemented in Europe, North America and Latin America, with increasingly diverse curricula on food processing and food technology. (HLPE, 2020[8]). Accurate profiling of youth will be important to capture different needs and challenges based on gender, age, education, wealth, ethnicity, health and geographic location. This will allow applying a youth lens to value chain/food system analysis and design targeted programmes (OECD, 2018[9]). Through careful targeting, programmes can for example offer youth aged 15-17 access to capacity-building and decent and age-appropriate work opportunities (FAO, 2018[10]).

The issue of informality needs to be addressed carefully because informal jobs in the agri-food sector sustains livelihoods of millions of vulnerable workers and formalising without adequate social protection will expose them to more difficult situations. Social protection to informal youth workers need to take the heterogeneity of this groups into account. Agriculture has higher work-related risks than jobs in the downstream segments of the food economy and social protection programmes should consider these aspects. Policies should look at how to build the capacity of entitlements as youth are more likely to fall into disguised employment relationships. Robust social protection systems must also recognise frequent movements among various forms of employment and ensure continued coverage. This can be achieved through better co-ordination of social insurance schemes and efforts to facilitate portability of entitlements between schemes (OECD/ILO, 2019[11]).

Overcoming environmental barriers

Agriculture is and will remain the main supplier of jobs in developing countries, particularly in sub-Saharan Africa and even in Southeast Asia, for some time to come. However, conventional farming practices through heavy use of chemical pesticides and fertilisers have been harmful to the environment in developed and developing countries alike. Alternative modes of production that are environmentally more sustainable need to be further explored. Several empirical studies on the potential of organic or agroecological agriculture (Aubert, 2009[12]; Badgley and Perfecto, 2007[13]; Halberg et al., 2006[14]; Stanhill, 1990[15]) find that large-scale conversion to organic agriculture would not severely diminish either the global food supply or food security in developing regions. The Halberg et al's study (2006[14]), which modelled scenarios of conversion to organic agriculture in Europe, North America and sub-Saharan Africa, using a globalised market model concludes that food policies favouring food availability, rather than export crops, would enhance the impact of conversion to organic farming and increase food security in sub-Saharan Africa. The issue of yield gap between organic and conventional farming keeps the opinions divided, however one thing is certain, sustainable food systems will need to address not only production methods but also food waste, crop-grass-livestock interdependencies and human consumption patterns (Muller et al., 2017[16]). At the same time, policies aimed at containing the adverse environmental effects of current agricultural production practices, such as more stringent regulatory procedures for use of harmful pesticides and chemical fertilisers, need to be further consolidated and enforced to achieve significant improvements in environmental outcomes of current production practices (OECD, 2021[17]).

Securing price premiums on agricultural products seems to be also a promising GVC upgrading option and so far the one that has proven to work for developing countries. There is evidence that price upgrade through organic farming and certification works. Organic agriculture is a rapidly growing sector in Africa, with strong links to economic and sociocultural development in the continent (Willer and Kilcher, 2012[18]; Auerbach et al., 2013[19]). Organic farming is also more labour intensive than regular farming. Organic agriculture can also be seen as a relevant tool to advance the Sustainable Development Goals (SDGs) 2, 12, 13 and 15 on sustainable agriculture, sustainable consumption and production, climate change and the sustainable use of ecosystems (UNCTAD, 2016[20]). Securing price premiums for organic products in export markets is one of the main drivers for the development of organic production in Africa, along with increased environmental sustainability and reduced dependence on external inputs (UNCTAD, 2009[21]). So far, export markets are regarded as the main destination of most certified African organic production. One of the best-documented illustrations of the export potential of African organic agriculture is the East Africa Export Programme (EAEP), which contributed to raise regional organic exports from USD 4.6 million in 2002-03 to USD 35 million in 2009-10. The EAEP led to the adoption of a common regional organic standard, the inclusion of organic products in national trade strategies and the development of supportive national policies and programmes. It also brought about a significant increase in average crop yields and the number of certified producers in Burundi, Kenya, Rwanda, Uganda and in the United Republic of Tanzania (UNCTAD, 2011[22]).

Recently, more holistic and multi-dimensional approaches that encompass the entirety of agriculture and food systems are being adopted. Agroecology is a concept that simultaneously applies ecological and social principles to the design and management of sustainable agriculture and food systems (FAO, n.d.[23]). It seeks to optimise the interactions between plants, animals, humans and the environment while also addressing the need for socially equitable food systems within which people can exercise choice over what they eat and how and where it is produced. Agroecology is based on applying ecological concepts and principles to optimise interactions between plants, animals, humans and the environment while taking into consideration the social aspects that need to be addressed for a sustainable and fair food system. By building synergies, agroecology can support food production and food security and nutrition while restoring the ecosystem services and biodiversity that are essential for sustainable agriculture. Agroecology can play an important role in building resilience and adapting to climate change (FAO, n.d.[23]). So far few studies exist on the impact of agroecology on labour. Bottazzi et al (2020[24]) looks at channels of labour control in agriculture based on four agroecological initiatives in Senegal. The study finds that despite the emphasis on improving farmers' well-being, without a holistic institutional backing to protect markets for their products and include farmers in the agro-ecosystem and take local communities into account, agroecological farming only becomes technical demonstrations rather than agents of transformation (Bottazzi et al., 2020[24]).

Table 5.1 below summarises some of the policy orientations countries could take to overcome the major bottlenecks and develop more vibrant local food economies.

Table 5.1. Overview of policy implications for local food economies

	Constraints	Bottlenecks	Policy directions
Economic	Low earnings for farmers and local food producers	Low productivity	Support mechanisation and technology transfer
		Poor market linkages	Improve rural-urban linkages, especially with secondary cities to create better access to local markets through better infrastructure and digital connectivity
		Low agricultural prices	Address unfair competition and price distortion by factoring in environmental externalities into final price
		Inconsistent quantity and quality of agricultural products or processed food by local SMEs	Support transfer of technologies and know-how in food processing, packaging and labelling, and marketing to ensure consistent quality and quantity of food products Develop transport and logistics for agri-food value chains, including storage and cold chain transport and distribution
		Lack of awareness or non-respect of food safety standards by local producers and processors	Strengthen phytosanitary and hygiene regulations, ensuring inclusive policies to support smallholder producers and processors Simplify hygiene regulations for informal markets Decrease compliance cost for smallholder producers
Social	Poor quality jobs in the food economy	High informality	Support local agribusinesses and high-potential youth entrepreneurs to grow their businesses and create more formal wage jobs through financial services (e.g. soft loans) and technology transfers and training Dialogue with the private sector and local SMEs to better understand labour market needs and link youth to internships and wage jobs Extend social protection to informal youth workers, taking into account the heterogeneity of work-related risks, disguised employment relationships and portability of social insurance entitlements between jobs
		Skills mismatch	Develop more training in agroecological practices and for jobs in downstream activities of the food economy Reform curricula in schools to include more agricultural sciences and food systems related subjects as well as soft skills development Profile youth to identify the different needs based on gender, age, education, wealth, ethnicity, health and geographic location and design programmes by applying a youth lens to value chain/food system analysis. Improve co-ordination between ministries of agriculture and rural development and those in charge of education and vocational training
Environmental	Environmental degradation from unsustainable agricultural practices	Low development of organic or agroecological practices in developing countries Low technological transfers	Promote organic or agroecological farming or conservation agriculture through more share of the agricultural subsidies or tax incentives Upgrade agricultural products through premium products (organic, fair trade certification) Promote territorial branding by improving knowledge of the market and marketing/branding strategies for local products, business development, utilisation of co-operative networks (support for marketing and branding) Engage local and regional authorities to 'champions' territorial development Increase environmentally-friendly technological transfers
		Poor consumer awareness of the benefits of farm-to-fork models and organic or agroecological farming	Raise consumer awareness for local, quality and organic products to create a market demand Improve public information about food safety certifications

Notes

[1] SDG goal 2: End hunger, achieve food security and improved nutrition and promote sustainable agriculture; SDG goal 8: Promote sustained, inclusive and sustainable growth, full and productive employment and decent work for all; SDG goal 12: Ensure sustainable consumption and production patterns.

References

AfDB et al. (2012), *African Economic Outlook 2012: Promoting Youth Employment*, OECD Publishing, Paris, https://dx.doi.org/10.1787/aeo-2012-en. [7]

Aubert, C. (2009), "Nourrir la planète avec l'agriculture biologique : mythe ou réalité ?", *Ecologie & politique*, Vol. N°38/1, http://dx.doi.org/10.3917/ecopo.038.0099. [12]

Auerbach et al. (2013), *Organic agriculture : African experiences in resilience and sustainability*, Natural Resources Management and Environment Dept., Food and Agriculture Organization of the United Nations. [19]

Badgley, C. and I. Perfecto (2007), "Can organic agriculture feed the world?", *Renewable Agriculture and Food Systems*, Vol. 22/2, http://dx.doi.org/10.1017/S1742170507001871. [13]

Bottazzi, P. et al. (2020), "Channels of labour control in organic farming: Toward a just agroecological transition for Sub-Saharan Africa", *Land*, Vol. 9/6, http://dx.doi.org/10.3390/LAND9060205. [24]

COGTA (2016), *2016 Integrated Urban Development Framework*, Ministry of Cooperative Governance and Traditional Affairs of South Africa, Pretoria. [5]

FAO (2018), *Promoting youth employment and reducing child labour in agriculture*, online course. [10]

FAO (n.d.), *Agroecology Knowledge Hub*. [23]

Government of Rwanda and GGGI (2015), *National Roadmap for Green Secondary City Development*, Global Green Growth Institute, Kigali. [4]

Halberg, N. et al. (eds.) (2006), *Global development of organic agriculture: challenges and prospects*, CABI, Wallingford, http://dx.doi.org/10.1079/9781845930783.0000. [14]

HLPE (2020), *Impacts of COVID-19 on food security and nutrition: developing effective policy responses to address the hunger and malnutrition pandemic*. [8]

Muller, A. et al. (2017), "Strategies for feeding the world more sustainably with organic agriculture", *Nature Communications*, Vol. 8/1, http://dx.doi.org/10.1038/s41467-017-01410-w. [16]

OECD (2021), *Making Better Policies for Food Systems*, OECD Publishing, Paris, https://dx.doi.org/10.1787/ddfba4de-en. [17]

OECD (2018), *The Future of Rural Youth in Developing Countries: Tapping the Potential of Local Value Chains*, OECD Publishing, Paris, https://doi.org/10.1787/9789264298521-en. [9]

OECD (2016), *A New Rural Development Paradigm for the 21st Century: A Toolkit for Developing Countries*, Development Centre Studies, OECD Publishing, Paris, https://doi.org/10.1787/9789264252271-en. [1]

OECD (forthcoming), *Intermediary Cities and Climate Change*, OECD, Paris. [3]

OECD/ILO (2019), *Tackling Vulnerability in the Informal Economy*, Development Centre Studies, OECD Publishing, Paris, https://dx.doi.org/10.1787/939b7bcd-en. [11]

OECD/PSI (2020), *Rural Development Strategy Review of Ethiopia: Reaping the Benefits of Urbanisation*, OECD Development Pathways, OECD Publishing, Paris, https://doi.org/10.1787/a325a658-en. [2]

Stanhill, G. (1990), "The comparative productivity of organic agriculture", *Agriculture, Ecosystems & Environment*, Vol. 30/1-2, http://dx.doi.org/10.1016/0167-8809(90)90179-H. [15]

UNCTAD (2016), *Financing Organic Agriculture in Africa: Mapping the issues*. [20]

UNCTAD (2011), *International Partnership for Sustainable Development: Promoting production and trade of organic agricultural products in East Africa*. [22]

UNCTAD (2009), "Sustaining African Agriculture Organic Production". [21]

UNIDO (2015), *Integrated Agro-Industrial Parks in Ethiopia*. [6]

Willer and Kilcher (2012), *The world of organic agriculture : statistics and emerging trends 2012*, IFOAM. [18]

Annex A. Methodological annex

A. Methodology for the descriptive statistics on youth employment in the food economy (Chapter 2)

Countries selected

The report provides an in-depth view on a diverse set of countries, which vary in their income levels, development, size and importance of the agricultural sector (as a percentage of gross domestic product, GDP), and business environment. Five of the countries are in sub-Saharan Africa and two are in Southeast Asia. Table A A.1 lists the sample countries and provides summary statistics for each, highlighting the report sample's heterogeneity. These countries represent a diverse set of agri-food producers, with varying levels of development, urbanisation and labour market dynamics.

Table A A.1. Descriptive information on countries in the study

	Year	World Bank income group	Urban population (%)	Agriculture (% of GDP)	Industry (% of GDP)	Services (% of GDP)	Agriculture land productivity in 2016 (constant 2004-06 USD)	Agriculture labour productivity in 2016 (constant 2004-06 USD)	Expected years of schooling (mean)	Youth unemployment rate (% of labour force aged 15-24)	Youth aged 15-29 (% of total population, 2015)
South Africa	2019	Upper middle	66.9	1.9	26.0	61.2	10.39	2 749.60	13.8	56.0	27.8
Namibia	2015	Upper middle	46.9	6.2	27.6	58.3	140.85	15 360.48	12.3	41.5	30.0
Zambia	2015	Lower middle	41.9	5.0	33.7	56.2	255.27	617.43	11.1	19.7	28.1
Tanzania	2014	Low	30.9	25.8	25.1	41.3	427.50	484.85	8.2	3.7	27.2
Uganda	2015	Low	22.1	23.6	26.4	42.8	92.17	598.03	11.2	2.6	28.0
Thailand	2017	Upper middle	49.2	8.4	35.1	56.5	1 473.98	2 726.71	14.7	4.4	20.6
Viet Nam	2016	Lower middle	34.5	16.3	32.7	40.9	2 738.45	1 441.67	12.7	7.0	26.1

Note: Except where specified, all information is provided for the year indicated in the second column. Countries are listed by region, then decreasing income level.
Sources: World Bank (2021[1]), World Development Indicators; UNDP (2020[2]) Human Development Index; UN DESA (2019[3]), 2019 World Population Prospects; IFPRI (2020[4]), Agricultural Total Factor Productivity (TFP), 2000-16 (dataset), https://datacatalog.worldbank.org/dataset/world-development-indicators.

Country profiles

South Africa

South Africa is an upper middle-income country with an economy largely based on services, manufacturing and mining (FAO, 2016[5]). While agriculture contributed only 1.9% of GDP and 5% of employment in 2019, South Africa has a highly developed and diversified agricultural sector, with climate conditions that are conducive to growing a variety of crops (World Bank, 2021[1]; US International Trade Administration, 2020[6]). Main commodities include maize, wheat, sugarcane, sunflower, potatoes, groundnuts, citrus and grapes. Close to half of the country's agricultural production value is derived from animal products. South Africa is a net exporter of food and primary agricultural products and imports processed foods. The agriculture sector is generally characterised by commercial farmers and subsistence smallholders engaging in intensive crop production and mixed farming, as well as cattle-ranching and sheep-farming (FAO, 2016[5]). The food economy in South Africa is diversified, with food manufacturing and services segments especially well developed, namely in the food retail sector, mostly dominated by large supermarket chains. The value added in services represents nearly 61.2% of GDP and 72.4% of employment (World Bank, 2021[1]). Recent years have seen the rise of large agri-businesses and agro-processors in the food systems value chain, with a decline in mid-sized farms and farmers increasingly engaged in contracts with supermarkets or processors at the expense of alternative market sources (Battersby, Marshak and Mngqibisa, 2016[7]).

Namibia

Namibia is an upper middle-income country. Agriculture is notoriously difficult in Namibia, as the country's climate is extremely arid. In 2019, agriculture represented 6.2% of the country's GDP and 21.8% of employment (World Bank, 2021[1]). Livestock farming constitutes approximately two-thirds of agricultural production and 24.5% of employment in agriculture, with crop farming and forestry making up the remaining production (US International Trade Administration, 2020[8]). Livestock also contributes to the majority of Namibia's exports by value, also around two-thirds, while the export value of crops has been rising in recent years (US International Trade Administration, 2021[9])Services are the country's main contributor to GDP as well as source of employment, with the value added in services representing 58.3% of GDP and the sector employing 61.7% of workers in 2019 (World Bank, 2021[1]).

Zambia

Zambia is a lower middle-income country. In 2015, Zambia's agricultural sector contributed only 5% to GDP but employed 51.7% of its workforce (World Bank, 2021[1]). Within the food economy, 89% of jobs are in agriculture, followed far behind by food trade (7.5%). Smallholder farms dominate the agricultural sector in Zambia, but a number of medium- and large-scale farms produce cash crops and other food items for domestic and export markets (Jayne et al., 2019[10]; US International Trade Administration, 2020[11]). The services economy, on the other hand, contributed 56.2% to GDP and employed 40% of the workforce in 2019 (World Bank, 2019[12]). Nutrient mining, soil erosion and poor water management continue to be the main constraints for further agricultural development and increased yields. It is estimated that, by 2025, maize production will decrease due to climate change, while the variability of yields may increase (FAO, 2021[13]).

Tanzania

Tanzania is a low-income country. Tanzania is heavily dependent on the agriculture sector which, in 2019, contributed 25.8% to its GDP and employed around 65% of its workers (World Bank, 2021[1]). The country's top commodities are primarily comprised of agricultural products, including cassava, maize, sweet potatoes and sugar cane (FAOSTAT, 2021[14]). Tanzanian farmers are shifting from smallholder and subsistence farming towards medium-scale and export-oriented production, and urban farming is increasing as well (Wineman et al., 2020[15]). Yet, productivity and the share of cultivated over arable land remain low, and farmers continue to rely on rain-fed agriculture and make use of limited modernised farming techniques (FAO, 2021[16]; WFP, 2021[17]). Tanzania has the third largest livestock population in Africa, as well as extensive natural resources for livestock development, including diverse vegetation and vast rangelands. In spite of these resources, the livestock sector is underperforming, as it only contributes 7.4% of the country's GDP and grows at a rate of 2.2% annually. Main constraints to growth include low livestock reproductive rates, high mortality and high disease prevalence. The services sector is growing, accounting for around 41.3% of GDP and approximately 28% of employment in 2019 (World Bank, 2021[1]). Moreover, the recent discovery of large natural gas and oil reserves presents the opportunity for new and significant sources of revenue for the country (WFP, 2021[17]).

Uganda

Uganda is a low-income country. Agriculture is the leading economic activity in Uganda, contributing 23.6% of GDP and 34% of its export earnings (US International Trade Administration, 2021[18]) and employing around 70% of its workers (World Bank, 2021[1]). Uganda's agricultural potential is considered to be among the best in Africa, as the country has low temperature variability, fertile soils and consistent rainy seasons, all of which lead to multiple crop harvests every year. The country's main agricultural products include coffee – of which Uganda is a leading exporter –, tea, sugar, livestock, fish, edible oils, cotton, tobacco, plantains, corn, beans, cassava, sweet potatoes, millet, sorghum and groundnuts. Currently, 80% of Uganda's land is arable but only 35% is cultivated. Farmers are almost entirely smallholders, making up 85% of the farming community, and are not scaling up (Anderson, Learch and Gardner, 2016[19]; World Bank, 2018[20]; Jayne et al., 2019[10]). They are also most vulnerable to climate change and will face challenges in terms of adaptation and sustainability (Atube et al., 2021[21]). Sector growth and commercialisation at the production level is inhibited by limited use of fertiliser and quality seeds and by a lack of infrastructure for irrigation. At the processing level, the low-quality packaging capabilities, few storage facilities, poor post-harvest handling practices, shortage of agricultural credit, high freight costs, a complicated and inefficient land tenure system, limited knowledge of modern production practices, and low-quality standards pose challenges to sector development and access to export markets. However, there are many opportunities for investment in Uganda's agriculture sector, notably in production, supply of inputs, value-added processing, standards compliance and export, and post-harvest handling (US International Trade Administration, 2021[18]). The services sector is growing, accounting for around 42.8% of GDP and about 21% of employment in 2019 (World Bank, 2021[1]).

Viet Nam

Viet Nam is a lower middle-income country with a rapidly developing economy, diminishing reliance on export-led agriculture, and rising economic growth due to industrialisation and services. Agriculture in Viet Nam benefitted from a Green Revolution, which saw advances in agricultural technologies that boosted factor productivity, such as irrigation techniques, seed varieties, fertiliser and pest control (Hazell, 2009[22]). Agriculture contributed to 16.3% of GDP and 37% of employment in 2019 (World Bank, 2021[1]), and the main commodities produced include rice, vegetables, sugar cane, cassava, maize, meat, fruit, bananas and coffee (FAOSTAT, 2019[23]). Commodities such as rice continue to be grown mainly by smallholders for local consumption, with only around 5% exported, while growing urban food markers have put increasing pressure on food production systems to modernise (GIZ, 2021[24]). Food trade is still an important feature in Viet Nam's food economy, providing about 13.4% of food economy jobs. In 2019, food manufacturing comprised 3.8% of food economy jobs in Viet Nam whereas food service jobs made up 4.9% of the country's food economy jobs. In general, services made up 40.9% of the country's GDP and 35% of its labour force (World Bank, 2021[1]).

Thailand

Thailand is an upper middle-income country. Agriculture only comprised 8.4% of Thailand's GDP and 31% of its total employment in 2019 (World Bank, 2021[1]). Food manufacturing comprised 6.2% of Thai food economy jobs, whereas food service jobs made up 10.5%. Similar to Viet Nam, agriculture in

Thailand benefited from a Green Revolution which modernised its agricultural practices (Hazell, 2009[22]). Sixty-eight percent of land for field crops is arable, and main commodities consist predominantly of sugar cane, followed by cassava, rice, palm oil, rubber, maize, fruit, meat and pineapples (FAOSTAT, 2019[25]; ITC, 2021[26]). Thailand is the largest exporter of tapioca products, rubber, frozen shrimp, canned tuna and canned pineapple in the world (US International Trade Administration, 2021[27]) and the agriculture sector largely consists of small-scale, family-owned and family-operated farms (FAOSTAT, 2019[25]). However, the agriculture sector generates the lowest value added per worker and exhibits the slowest growth relative to other economic sectors (UN Thailand, 2020[28]); it has largely been overtaken by services, Thailand's main sector of economic activity, which makes up 56.5% of its GDP and 46% of its workforce (World Bank, 2021[1]).

Data source

Household surveys were used to produce the analysis in Chapter 1, with the exception of South Africa where a labour force survey was used. Table A A.2 lists the data sources for each sample country. Unless stated otherwise, figures provided throughout the chapter for each country correspond to the year of the survey in question.

Table A A.2. List of sample countries

	Year	Survey source
South Africa	2019	Labour Market Dynamics South Africa/Quarterly Labour Force Survey, Q1-Q4
Namibia	2015	Namibia Household Income and Expenditure Survey
Zambia	2015	Living Conditions Monitoring Survey
Tanzania	2014	National Panel Survey
Uganda	2015	National Panel Survey
Thailand	2017	Socio-Economic Survey
Viet Nam	2016	Household Living Standards Survey

Definitions

Employment in the food economy is assigned using the information from the United Nations International Standard Industrial Classification of All Economic Activities (ISIC) that accompanies each job. Following the classification scheme outlined in Allen et al. (2016[29]) and Allen, Heinrigs and Heo (2018[30]), the food economy has been grouped into the following four broad categories:

1. **Food agriculture**: activities within the primary sector dedicated to the production of agricultural and animal products for human consumption (ISIC divisions 1, 3)
2. **Food processing**: activities related to processing and manufacturing food and beverages for human consumption (ISIC divisions 10, 11, 12)
3. **Food marketing**: all transport, wholesale and retail activities related to food (ISIC codes 4653, 4711, 472, 4781).
4. **Food-away-from-home**: restaurants, street food and other catering services (ISIC division 56).

As the ISIC categorisation scheme does not sufficiently disaggregate between the types of cargo transported, isolating food-related transport was not possible. An adjustment was made for the estimates on food-related transportation, using aggregate food expenditure as a proxy for the aggregate food demand of the country in question. Estimates of aggregate food demand were made using a national average of food consumption in total consumption taken from household surveys in the same year for each sample country.

For certain parts of the analysis, a full-time equivalent (FTE) method of defining jobs was used. This method defines one FTE as 40 hours worked per week and estimates employment by converting the total number of hours worked into the number of FTE jobs (that are equal to one full-time equivalent in employment). Full-time employment is defined over the course of one calendar year (52 weeks). Full-time equivalents were generated based on the number of hours worked per week per job, over the course of 52 weeks.

"Youth" refers to young women and young men between the ages of 15 and 29. "Adults" refers to all those aged above 29. "Working-age population" refers to all those aged above 15.

B. Methodology for the employment forecasting (Chapter 3)

Chapter 2 sought to contribute to our understanding of the employment potential in the food economy by forecasting the changes in employment directly associated with rapid urbanisation and the rise of the middle class, holding all else constant. The projections show that such trends would increase the overall level of employment in the food economy, in absolute terms in the case of agriculture and, in the case of downstream segments, in both absolute and relative terms. Looking at the changes within the different segments of the food economy further shows a rebalancing of food economy employment from the agricultural sector to secondary and tertiary food economy activities.

All in all, these results suggest that if local food systems were to take on the challenge of responding to higher and changing domestic demand for food, a large number of new jobs could be created in the food economy. Chapter 3 discussed how different types of local food systems could further influence the quantity and quality of employment in the food economy, while responding to the social, economic and environmental challenges.

This forecasting exercise is based on two novel, uniquely disaggregated sectoral employment datasets provided by the International Labour Organization (ILO): Employment by sex and economic activity (ILO modelled estimates) and Employment by sex and economic activity (ISIC level 2).

A two-step methodology was specifically developed to harness information from both datasets, using GDP and urbanisation as main predictors and deriving country-specific elasticities. Employment estimates at horizon 2030 relied on the United Nations' (UN) *2018 Revision of World Urbanization Prospects* (available at horizon 2030) and the International Monetary Fund's (IMF) *World Economic Outlook* GDP forecasts (available at horizon 2025, extended to 2030; see Annex A for details).

Estimation step 1: Broad sectors

Employment-growth and employment-urban population partial elasticities are the first set of parameters used to produce employment projections for the food economy. Employment elasticities measure the employment "intensity" or sensitivity of, in our case, economic growth and urbanisation. They provide important information about labour markets and serve as an indicator of how growth in economic output and growth in employment evolve together over time.

In a first step, country-specific long-term elasticities are estimated for four broad sectors of the economy:

- Agriculture; forestry and fishing (ISIC 4.0, letter A)
- Manufacturing (ISIC 4.0, letter C)
- Wholesale and retail trade; repair of motor vehicles and motorcycles (ISIC 4.0, letter G)
- Accommodation and food service activities (ISIC 4.0, letter I).

Following the IMF guidelines for forecasting labour market indicators (Chami, 2012[31]), we estimate the following for each country separately:

$$\ln(empl_{i,s,t}^{BROAD}) = \alpha_i + X\beta_{i,s} + \varepsilon_{i,t}$$

where $empl_{i,s,t}$ is the employment of sector s in country i at time t.

X is a matrix of explanatory variables, $X = [\ln GDP\ ;\ \ln UrbanPop]$.

The specification is estimated separately for each country/sector over the 1990-2019 period, therefore obtaining country/sector specific parameters $\beta_{i,s}$, the elasticity of employment of sector s in i with respect to GDP and urban population (absolute level). These regressors are mainly to be interpreted as "demand" factors, as GDP growth and urbanisation are key determinants of an increase in food demand and related labour demand. Yet, they also pick up labour market supply, as urban population level is correlated with overall population level, for example. The estimation uses robust standard errors.

Employment data are obtained from the ILO's modelled estimates, providing information on sector-level employment for all countries. GDP is obtained from the World Bank's *World Development Indicators*, and urbanisation is obtained from the UN's *2018 Revision of World Urbanization Prospects*.

Estimation step 2: Specific sectors

In a second step, a relationship between the broad sectors and the specific food economy sectors is estimated in a panel setting, exploiting the highly disaggregated Employment by sex and economic activity (ISIC level 2), recently released by the ILO. The following specification is applied:

$$\ln(empl_{i,s,t}^{SPECIFIC}) = \alpha_i + \sum_{r \in R} \beta_{r,s} \ln(empl_{i,s,t}^{BROAD}) + \epsilon_{i,st}$$

where $empl_{i,s,t}^{SPECIFIC}$ is the specific two-digit sector, for example Restaurants (ISIC 4.0 division 56), $empl_{i,s,t}^{BROAD}$ is the broad sector containing the specific sector, in this case Accommodation and food service activities (ISIC 4.0, letter I). $\beta_{r,s}$ corresponds to region X income group specific parameters, estimated for each sector s. The estimation clusters standard errors at the country level.

The projected employment growth is given by the following expression:

$$\Delta \ln(\widetilde{empl_{i,s,t}^{SPECIFIC}}) = \beta_{r,s} \cdot \sum_{x \in X} \beta_{i,s} \cdot \Delta x$$

Where X is the set of step-1 regressors.

Future gross domestic product and urbanisation

The baseline scenarios are built around extensions of the IMF's *World Economic Outlook* (October 2020) forecasts, with the baseline scenario assuming that countries return to their long-term, pre-COVID growth path.

We articulate scenarios around the *World Economic Outlook* forecast (IMF, 2020[32]) October update, which provides growth forecasts at horizon 2025.

For our baseline scenario, we assume that countries will grow until 2025 at the rates forecasted by the IMF. Beyond 2025, we assume that countries will return to a pre-pandemic "long-term growth path". We define the long-term path as the average growth between 2014 and 2024 as forecasted by the IMF in 2019 (IMF, 2020[32]).

References

Allen, A. et al. (2016), *Agrifood Youth Employment and Engagement Study (AgYEES)*, Michigan State University, East Lansing, Michigan. [29]

Allen, T., P. Heinrigs and I. Heo (2018), "Agriculture, Food and Jobs in West Africa", *West African Papers*, No. 14, OECD Publishing, Paris, https://dx.doi.org/10.1787/dc152bc0-en. [30]

Anderson, J., C. Learch and S. Gardner (2016), *National Survey and Segmentation of Smallholder Households in Uganda: Understanding Their Demand for Financial, Agricultural, and Digital Solutions*. [19]

Atube, F. et al. (2021), "Determinants of smallholder farmers' adaptation strategies to the effects of climate change: Evidence from northern Uganda", *Agriculture & Food Security*, Vol. 10/6, pp. 1-14, http://dx.doi.org/10.1186/s40066-020-00279-1. [21]

Battersby, J., M. Marshak and N. Mngqibisa (2016), *No. 05: Mapping the Informal Food Economy in Cape Town, South Africa*, http://scholars.wlu.ca/hcp (accessed on 15 January 2019). [7]

Chami, R. (2012), "A Template for Analyzing and Projecting Labor Market Indicators", *Technical Notes and Manuals*, Vol. 12/01, http://dx.doi.org/10.5089/9781475522051.005. [31]

FAO (2021), *Economics and Policy Innovations for Climate-Smart Agriculture- Zambia*, http://www.fao.org/climatechange/epic/projects/countries/zambia/en/ (accessed on 5 July 2021). [13]

FAO (2021), *FAO in Tanzania*, http://www.fao.org/tanzania/fao-in-tanzania/tanzania-at-a-glance/en/ (accessed on 28 June 2021). [16]

FAO (2016), *Country Profile- South Africa*, FAO, Rome, Italy, http://dx.doi.org/10.21552/cclr/2010/4/146. [5]

FAOSTAT (2021), *Commodities By Country: Tanzania*, http://www.fao.org/faostat/en/#rankings/commodities_by_country. [14]

FAOSTAT (2019), *Commodities by country - Thailand*, http://faostat.fao.org/site/339/default.aspx. [25]

FAOSTAT (2019), *Commodities by country - Viet Nam*, http://faostat.fao.org/site/339/default.aspx. [23]

GIZ (2021), *Better Rice , Better Life*. [24]

Hazell, P. (2009), *The Asian Green Revolution*, International Food Policy Research Institute (IFPRI), Washington, DC, http://www.ifpri.org/millionsfed (accessed on 3 May 2021). [22]

IFPRI (2020), *Agricultural Total Factor Productivity (TFP), 2000-2016*, International Food Policy Research Institute, Washington, DC. [4]

IMF (2020), *World Economic Outlook, October 2020*, International Monetary Fund Research Department, Washington, DC, http://dx.doi.org/10.5089/9781513556055.081. [32]

ITC (2021), *Country profile - Thailand*, https://www.intracen.org/exporters/organic-products/country-focus/Country-Profile-Thailand/ (accessed on 5 July 2021). [26]

Jayne, T. et al. (2019), "Are medium-scale farms driving agricultural transformation in sub-Saharan Africa?", *Agricultural Economics*, Vol. 50, pp. 75-95, http://dx.doi.org/10.1111/agec.12535. [10]

UN DESA (2019), *2019 Revision of World Population Prospects*, United Nations Department of Economic and Social Affairs, New York, https://population.un.org/wpp/ (accessed on 12 February 2021). [3]

UN Thailand (2020), *Thai Agricultural Sector: From Problems to Solutions*, https://thailand.un.org/en/103307-thai-agricultural-sector-problems-solutions (accessed on 5 July 2021). [28]

UNDP (2020), *Human Development Index (HDI)*, United Nations Development Programme, http://hdr.undp.org/en/content/human-development-index-hdi (accessed on 12 February 2021). [2]

US International Trade Administration (2021), *Namibia - Country Commercial Guide*, https://www.trade.gov/country-commercial-guides/namibia-agricultural-sector (accessed on 29 June 2021). [9]

US International Trade Administration (2021), *Thailand- Country Commercial*, https://www.trade.gov/country-commercial-guides/thailand-agriculture (accessed on 5 July 2021). [27]

US International Trade Administration (2021), *Uganda- Country Commercial Guide*, https://www.trade.gov/country-commercial-guides/uganda-agricultural-sector (accessed on 5 July 2021). [18]

US International Trade Administration (2020), *Namibia - Country Commercial Guide- Agricultural Sector*, International Trade Administration, Department of Commerce, United States, https://www.trade.gov/country-commercial-guides/namibia-agricultural-sector (accessed on 30 April 2021). [8]

US International Trade Administration (2020), *South Africa - Country Commercial Guide - Agricultural Sector*, International Trade Administration, Department of Commerce, United States, https://www.trade.gov/knowledge-product/south-africa-agricultural-sector (accessed on 30 April 2021). [6]

US International Trade Administration (2020), *Zambia - Country Commercial Guide - Agriculture Sector*, International Trade Administration, Department of Commerce, United States, https://www.trade.gov/country-commercial-guides/zambia-agriculture (accessed on 2 May 2021). [11]

WFP (2021), *WFP Tanzania Country Brief May 2021*, WFP, https://docs.wfp.org/api/documents/WFP-0000129056/download/?_ga=2.16700211.465896956.1624895429-2141713910.1622558541. [17]

Wineman, A. et al. (2020), "The changing face of agriculture in Tanzania: Indicators of transformation", *Development Policy Review*, Vol. 38/6, pp. 685-709, http://dx.doi.org/10.1111/dpr.12491. [15]

World Bank (2021), *World Development Indicators (WDI)*, World Bank, Washington, DC, https://datacatalog.worldbank.org/dataset/world-development-indicators (accessed on 6 December 2018). [1]

World Bank (2020), *World Development Indicators*, The World Bank Group. [33]

World Bank (2019), *World Development Indicators*, The World Bank Group. [12]

World Bank (2018), *Closing the Potential-Performance Divide in Ugandan Agriculture*, World Bank, Washington, DC, http://www.worldbank.org (accessed on 2 May 2021). [20]

www.ingramcontent.com/pod-product-compliance
Ingram Content Group UK Ltd.
Pitfield, Milton Keynes, MK11 3LW, UK
UKHW050413240426
12048UKWH00020B/1483